Parliament, the Budget and Poverty in South Africa:

A Shift in Power

Edited by Len Verwey

with Kate Lefko-Everett, Ahmed Mohamed, and Musa Zamisa

idasa

AN AFRICAN DEMOCRACY INSTITUTE

2009

Idasa is an independent public interest organisation committed to promoting sustainable democracy based on active citizenship, democratic institutions and social justice.

The Budget Unit of Idasa's Political Information and Monitoring Service (PIMS) engages in research and advocacy on the role of economic policy in alleviating poverty, reducing inequality and unemployment and contributing to the realisation of socio-economic rights.

For further information on the Unit's work please visit our page on the Idasa website: www.idasa.org or contact Len Verwey: 021 467 7601, lverwey@idasa.org.za

Published by Idasa, 357 Visagie Street, Pretoria 0002

© Idasa 2009

ISBN 978-1-920118-91-4

First published 2009

Copy-edited by Drew Forrest

Cover by Mandy Darling, Magenta Media

Layout by Bronwen Müller, Idasa Publishing

Production by Idasa Publishing

Bound and printed by ABC Press, Cape Town

FOREWORD

In April 2009, President Kgalema Motlanthe, the third president of democratic South Africa, signed a bill into law allowing Parliament to amend the national budget. This was the culmination of a campaign by unions, civil society organisations and political parties to create budget amendment powers for Parliament, a campaign that began at the birth of the democratic dispensation.

For this reason, *Parliament, the Budget and Poverty in South Africa: A Shift in Power* is a timely book.

It originated in a multi-stakeholder symposium convened by Idasa in 2008 to reflect on key elements of what has now become the Money Bills Amendment Procedure and Related Matters Act (No 9 of 2009). The book provides a further assessment of the Act and identifies some of what is required if its provisions are to improve the quality and impact of the budget.

The editors have, however, a more important goal than helping to ensure an efficient and effective budget. This publication emerges from a particular context – South Africa's widespread, intractable poverty, exacerbated by islands of plenty.

Democracies which have many poor people may survive institutionally, but those afflicted by great inequality and relative deprivation face special challenges. And the question must be asked: how valuable is a constitutional democracy which cannot improve the quality of life of its citizens and enable them to prosper and participate fully in the economic and political life that is under construction? The question is particularly relevant where adequate resources do seem to exist, as in South Africa.

South Africa has not had an explicit, publicly negotiated poverty reduction strategy. Instead, it has relied on the medium-term expenditure framework and government programmes of action to structure interventions, foster debate and secure social ownership of state initiatives. To date, public participation has been fairly weak and tensions have regularly surfaced over aspects of the budget, including its macro-economic stance and the effective spending of allocations.

As the country's fourth presidency gets under way and the fourth Parliament convenes, there is an opportunity to re-establish the primacy of citizen agency in public finances. The new amendment powers clearly give non-governmental stakeholders a positive incentive to engage with the budget. But having these powers is not the same as exercising them wisely and in favour of the poor.

In the realm of budgeting, we may have arrived at a new moment in South Africa's democratic journey. This publication reminds us of where we have come from and sketches a map that can be used in navigating the immediate future. As always, underlying these pressing, sometimes technical issues is the need for South Africans to further the promise that we make every time we celebrate the Constitution: to "improve the quality of life of all citizens and free the potential of each person".

Paul Graham, Executive Director: Idasa
September 2009

CONTENTS

Contributors

Tania Ajam

Tania Ajam is a public finance economist with broad experience in the design, analysis and implementation of fiscal policy, intergovernmental fiscal relations and sectoral public budget management. She is director of the knowledge centre at the Applied Fiscal Research Centre (Pty) Ltd (AFReC), a training and consulting company affiliated to the University of Cape Town. She is also the managing director of PBS (Pty) Ltd, which implements performance budgeting systems. Tania also serves on the Financial and Fiscal Commission.

Kate Lefko-Everett

Kate Lefko-Everett is the project leader of the reconciliation barometer at the Institute for Justice and Reconciliation. From 2004-2009 she worked as a researcher for Idasa's Southern African Migration Project and Political Information and Monitoring Service (PIMS) where her research focused on poverty and inequality, social security, governance and the public service.

Ahmed Mohamed

Ahmed Mohamed worked as a budget researcher in Idasa's PIMS in 2008 and 2009. He is currently the parliamentary information and monitoring manager for Equal Education, a Cape Town-based NGO which advocates for quality and equal education in South Africa.

Len Verwey

Len Verwey manages the Budget Unit of Idasa's PIMS. His research has included work on budgeting and socio-economic rights, the role of Parliament in the budget, political economic debates in South Africa and their budgetary implications, and the challenges of budgeting at sub-national level in South Africa. He has coordinated Idasa's responses to the South African Budget and Medium-Term Budget Policy Statement in recent years.

Joachim Wehner

Dr Joachim Wehner is a lecturer in public policy at the London School of Economics and Political Science, where he is also a member of the public policy group and the political science and political economy research group. Previously, he worked at

Idasa's Budget Information Service. His research interests include comparative public budgeting, fiscal performance and decentralisation. He is completing a book on legislatures and the budget process.

Musa Zamisa

Musa Zamisa is a researcher in the PIMS Budget Unit at Idasa. His research focuses on aspects of participatory budgeting in the South African environment. His research has included work on the importance of participatory budgeting for socio-economic development and the achievement of greater social justice.

Acknowledgements

As with all books, this publication would not have been possible without the support of a number of people and institutions.

Firstly, our sincere thanks to the Embassy of the Kingdom of the Netherlands, Pretoria, for their funding of Idasa's Political Information and Monitoring Service, which made this publication possible.

We are also very grateful to Idasa's Publishing Department for their enthusiasm, hard work and high levels of professionalism.

This project benefited considerably from the guidance, support and, where needed, highly active involvement of Judith February, the PIMS Programme Manager. Thank you.

Lastly, our thanks to Paul Graham, Executive Director of Idasa, for writing the foreword and providing useful comments at various stages of the process.

The Editors
September 2009

Introduction

Kate Lefko-Everett, Ahmed Mohamed,
Len Verwey, Musa Zamisa

Since the transition to democracy in 1994, South Africa has undergone considerable self-assessment and restructuring. In addition to a range of social and economic challenges that had to be urgently addressed, it was also necessary to bring about the fundamental restructuring of democratic institutions and the public sector.

Fiscal governance in the apartheid era was largely non-transparent and broader mechanisms of accountability and citizen participation did not exist. Neither Parliament nor civil society organisations were actively involved in decision-making processes, including those relating to budgeting. Even within the cabinet, budget information appears to have been selectively available to ministers, with many items, such as those pertaining to defence and internal security, shrouded in secrecy.

Lack of transparency, combined with the unwieldy apartheid bureaucracy, the absence of centralised expenditure monitoring and the practice of in-year resource diversion, meant that spending and budget outcomes often differed markedly from budgetary intentions. Large unintended deficits, for example, indicated failures of the budget system as an instrument of financial management and control, as well as reflecting the dire state of the South African economy.

Since 1994, the government, led by the African National Congress (ANC), has worked to build a more transparent, accountable and participatory system of fiscal governance. The foundations of such reforms were laid by the 1996 Constitution, which also recognised Parliament and civil society as key players in democratic budgeting processes. In recognition of the interests of civil society, for instance, sections 59 and 72 of the Constitution require both houses of Parliament, the National Assembly and the National Council of Provinces (NCOP), to facilitate public involvement in their legislative processes. The National Assembly and the NCOP are further required to conduct their business in an open manner. Section 195 further demands that when matters of public administration are considered "people's needs must be responded to, and the public must be encouraged to participate in decision-making".

The 1996 Constitution also clearly recognises the balance of power between Parliament and the executive arm of government. Section 55 (1) and 144 (1) give the National Assembly and provincial legislatures the power to "consider, pass, amend or reject any legislation" prepared by the executive. This includes any budget-related legislation, referred to as "money bills". Sections 55 (2) and 144 (2) empower both the National Assembly and NCOP to hold the executive to account, and to scrutinise and oversee implementation. Both national and provincial legislatures are, therefore, given the authority to engage with budget policy and oversee the implementation of budgets.

The Public Finance Management Act and the Municipal Finance Management Act also embody rigorous requirements for reporting, tendering and the performance of accounting officers. This reflects a shift away from a narrow emphasis on accountability for financial regularity towards a results orientation. Accounting officers have been given greater managerial discretion to structure their programmes to meet policy objectives. National Assembly and NCOP legislators and committees have, in turn, had to improve their capacity for effective oversight.

However, these reforms have primarily expanded *ex post facto* oversight, that is oversight of budget implementation. Parliament has lacked the formal power to amend budgets required by section 77 of the Constitution, which mandates the passing of an Act of Parliament that sets out a procedure for the legislative amendment of money bills. Despite a number of attempts to introduce such legislation, it has not been passed into law. A draft bill circulated in 1997 ran into strong opposition, as it significantly constrained the role of Parliament in budgeting.

In 2008, however, the Money Bills Amendment Procedure and Related Matters Bill (B75-2008) was introduced. By early 2009, the bill had passed through both houses of Parliament, and days before the 2009 elections, President Kgalema Motlanthe signed it into law as the Money Bills Amendment Procedure and Related Matters Act (No 9 of 2009).

The new version of the bill and its relatively rapid progress through the legislative mill can be ascribed to the belief among legislators and civil society that the executive dominated budgetary decision-making to an excessive degree. Also influential were political power shifts in the ANC after the party's 52nd national conference in Polokwane in 2007.

The Polokwane conference saw a resurgence of the "left" in the ANC and its partners in the tripartite alliance, the Congress of South African Trade Unions (Cosatu) and the South African Communist Party (SACP). Both organisations have lobbied for a more assertive Parliament and in particular, strong legislative powers to amend budgets. The draft bill went through various rewrites in 2008 and public hearings were held in August of that year[1]. By the end of this process, most stakeholders seemed fairly satisfied, although some concerns were raised about Parliament's ability to give meaningful effect to the budgetary powers now conferred on it.

The Act gives Parliament relatively unrestricted power to amend the budget, including the fiscal framework, the division of revenue (DoR), specific allocations and tax policy. It does, however, require Parliament to consider a range of factors in proposing amendments. Specific sequencing is also required: the fiscal framework must be accepted or amended before the DoR is considered, which in turn must be accepted or amended before particular allocations are considered, and so on. In this way, the Act tries to ensure that amendments to allocations remain consistent with the fiscal framework and that a proliferation of vote amendments do not result in an unsustainable fiscal policy stance.

The Act further provides for the establishment of a Parliamentary Budget Office (PBO) to provide independent and non-partisan research, expertise and advice. Parliamentarians and committees had previously had the benefit of some research support through the parliamentary research office and committee researchers, but no dedicated support on budget matters was available. The establishment of the PBO will improve Parliament's institutional capacity, in turn enhancing its oversight abilities.

While the Act contains a number of provisions that empower Parliament, it also creates significant scope for public participation, especially during the legislative phase of the budget process.

The powers conferred by the Act, in conjunction with the oversight powers that already existed, give Parliament a strong opportunity to assert itself in budgeting and spending matters. In addition, Parliament could potentially play a significant role in assessing the extent to which budgetary expenditure achieves public objectives. The interrelated challenges of poverty, inequality and unemployment in South Africa remain urgent and acute, despite the real progress made in these areas since 1994.

This book focuses on Parliament's new budgetary amendment powers, its oversight role and its ability to alleviate poverty through the budget. Given the formal powers assigned to Parliament, it can clearly play a significant role in ensuring that fiscal policy embodies appropriate trade-offs between sustainability and measures that address urgent challenges; that allocations mirror social preferences and target the poor and other vulnerable groups; and that money is spent with the minimum of waste. When these requirements are not met, Parliament must intervene. As discussed throughout this book, however, parliamentary intervention must satisfy a number of criteria if it is to improve budgetary outcomes.

It is important to note that Parliament's role in the budget must go beyond narrow oversight. It must provide a genuinely public and participatory space for understanding the complex and multi-dimensional nature of poverty in South Africa, and for working with the poor in planning and prioritising social spending. Such an approach is both democratic and economically prudent. Worldwide, the experience has been that participatory budgets are more likely to result in efficient allocation, as they are based on an understanding of the needs and experiences of the recipients of public goods and services. Furthermore, effective public participation gives rise to greater social ownership of the budget, which in turn improves scrutiny of spending and reduces corrosive conflict over public resources.

To explore these questions further, Idasa hosted a multi-stakeholder symposium that brought together Members of Parliament, civil society organisations, academics and the media in October 2008. Participants agreed that the budgetary authority given to Parliament by the new legislation was far-reaching and met the requirements of the Constitution. However, there was also agreement that a number of conditions would have to be met for this formal authority to translate into improved budget policy and outcomes. These key issues – the quality of the legislation and the necessary conditions for its effective realisation – are central to this book.

In Chapter 1, Len Verwey discusses key aspects of pro-poor budgeting and related budget reform and reviews poverty trends in South Africa. He then assesses budgeting performance in South Africa, and identifies challenges that Parliament must continue to grapple with.

In Chapter 2, Joachim Wehner traces the history of the budgetary amendment legislation in South Africa, from the draft tabled in 1997 to the 2009 Act. The chapter then presents the findings of a 2003 study on legislative powers in budgeting in more than 30 countries, concluding that South Africa was among the weakest because it lacked amendment powers. The chapter also evaluates whether the 2008 bill embodies the procedural safeguards needed to ensure fiscal responsibility in the context of amendment powers.

Chapter 3 focuses on effective in-year parliamentary oversight and its crucial role in shaping the budget for the purposes of poverty alleviation. Tania Ajam discusses how strong budgetary oversight in Parliament could create incentives for public institutions to be effective, efficient and responsive to the needs of the poor.

Chapter 4, by Ahmed Mohamed, discusses the Parliamentary Budget Office required by the Act and its role in parliamentary oversight of the budget. The chapter outlines the proposed functions of the budget office and reviews the useful support it could provide. It also looks at the necessary conditions for effective institutional performance.

In Chapter 5, Kate Lefko-Everett and Musa Zamisa examine the new opportunities created by the Act for public participation in budgeting, specifically at the national level in Parliament. The authors analyse public participation in Parliament's Portfolio Committee on Finance as a case study, finding that the new Act presents opportunities for more meaningful public participation in future. However, they also argue that much will depend on how Parliament and civil society use these opportunities.

Chapter 1

Pro-poor budgeting: general reflections and the South African situation

Len Verwey

1. INTRODUCTION[2]

The ANC government that came to power in 1994, after the country's first democratic elections, faced a range of social, economic and institutional challenges. These included high levels of inequality, poverty and unemployment, an economy which had performed poorly in preceding years, precarious public finances resulting from a high debt burden, and a cumbersome bureaucracy which required a fundamental overhaul if it was to give effect to the policy objectives of the new government.

The defining budgetary challenge of the initial post-democratic period lay in meeting the urgent needs of the time while simultaneously trying to place public finances on a more secure footing. The South African experience has acutely reflected many of the debates and tensions which arise from defining and implementing budgets that are truly "pro-poor" – that is, leave poor people significantly better off than they would have been otherwise.

To make an impact on poverty, any pro-poor budget must meet a number of criteria, and in practice, governments and other stakeholders do not necessarily give adequate emphasis to them all. The budget must, in the first place, embody an appropriate trade-off between longer-term sustainability and shorter-term interventions. Erring either on the side of excessive caution or an excessive appetite for fiscal risk is likely to have a disproportionately detrimental impact on poor households. A pro-poor budget must also be characterised by allocative and operational efficency.[3] From a governance perspective, the budget system should be sufficiently transparent and participatory to ensure that it responds to the revealed preferences of citizens, while there should be adequate mechanisms of accountability to ensure that those responsible for spending do not waste resources. Budgeting failures can generally be attributed to lack of capacity or a lack of adequate performance incentives for those who make and implement policy. It is important for oversight bodies to determine which of these is the main culprit in a given context.

Poverty is one of three major, interrelated challenges in South Africa that the budget has to address, together with unemployment and inequality. Most evidence suggests that there was little change in headcount income poverty rates in the country between 1994 and 2001. Nor does it appear that the depth of income poverty diminished significantly over this period. However, the post-2001 period has seen higher economic growth rates and significant job creation. With the resulting growth in government revenue, social spending, including social grants programmes, has also expanded. The impact on poverty rates has been unambiguously positive.

Nevertheless, poverty rates remain high in South Africa, and it is unlikely that grants will grow beyond envisaged adjustments in the age thresholds for the state pension and the child support grant.[4] Recently, there have been proposals of a wage subsidy to facilitate access to a compulsory contributory state pension fund, and if this materialises, it may also have an impact on poverty. However, there can be little doubt that further significant poverty reduction will have to be be achieved mainly by reducing unemployment and making the budget more operationally efficient.

In the remainder of this chapter, these questions are given further consideration. The aim of the chapter is to provide a broad sketch of current circumstances and challenges in budgeting in South Africa, and to touch on some of the theoretical questions involved. It is hoped that the discussion will form a useful backdrop to the more detailed treatment of Parliament's role in budgeting for poverty alleviation in later chapters.

2. ASPECTS OF PRO-POOR BUDGETING

Poverty can be most simply understood and measured as a condition in which people lack sufficient income to buy the goods and services they need to sustain themselves in a socially appropriate manner. As a point of departure in assessing the depth and breadth of poverty in a particular country, this remains a useful definition. However, in recent decades there has been a practical and theoretical shift towards understanding poverty as a more complex phenomenon. More than monetary income, for example, is required for well-being or the elimination of what Amartya Sen calls "capabilities deprivation".[5] Factors such as race, sex and location play a significant part in determining the extent to which income contributes to the realisation of positive freedoms.[6] It is widely recognised that countries with similar per capita incomes can score differently on development indicators such as life expectancy, educational attainment and maternal mortality.[7] There may be similar disparities between regions in many countries, as well as between rural and urban populations in a given region.

Furthermore, any analysis of poverty which restricts itself to *earned* income misses the potentially large impact of social, political, cultural and geographical factors on the well-being of households, as well as the impact of publicly provided goods and services and subsidised access to assets such as housing.[8]

In recent years, there has also been a growing focus on the behavioural incentives of the poor and on what might be called the subjective or "lived" experience of poverty. In a review of changing conceptions of poverty, Kanbur et al. note that "as we learn more about and from the poor, the concept has developed further to reflect a concern with vulnerability and risk, and with powerlessness and lack of voice". (Kanbur, R.and Squire, L., 1999:1) From a policy perspective, it is vital to have useable information on income poverty and broader capability deprivation, but it is equally important to have a sense of what keeps people poor in a given social and economic context. Where, for example, severe gender bias defines the relationship between men and women, direct income transfers to the household head may do little to improve the circumstances of women and girls. Similarly, traditional models of economic growth generally place a heavy emphasis on the role of entrepreneurs in identifying new opportunities to meet demand and in taking on financial risk in expectation of a financial return. But the risks of failure for the poor are often so prohibitive that there is, unsurprisingly, little evidence of entrepreneurship in the absence of risk-sharing schemes, concessional credit and similar mechanisms.

How one understands poverty, and the importance one attaches to reducing income poverty as the fundamental aim of development, are clearly of more than academic interest. How poverty is conceptualised and what one regards as its main causes (the nature of the "poverty discourse", in other words) has significant implications for the importance attached to poverty reduction initiatives, for the kinds of programmes likely to be funded through the budget in the name of poverty alleviation, and for the criteria used in determining whether they have succeeded. For example, there will be less support for social assistance programmes in a context where poverty is regarded mainly as a failure of individual initiative and entrepreneurship, and where the severity of the "poverty trap" is downplayed, than one in which poverty is seen as a result of structural factors beyond the control of individuals and where the obstacles to overcoming poverty are seen as difficult to surmount. As discussed in subsequent chapters,[9] the formal scope for participation provided by legislatures is vital to understanding the nature of poverty in a particular country and the experiences and needs of the poor themselves, as well as in arriving at "multi-dimensional" solutions which embody a high degree of social ownership.

One practical benefit, however, of relying on income adequacy as a central indicator of poverty and deprivation is that researchers have access to more useable and comparable information. More complex composite indicators that seek to reflect the multi-dimensionality of poverty are more open to conceptual contestation, less comparable across data-sets, and are likely to be more information-intensive. A further reason for retaining a primary focus on income, while broadening the analysis when necessary, is that people who are identified as poor in terms of income are, more often than not, also identified as poor when other measures are used. (Kanbur, R.and Squire, L., 1999: 1,2)

A pro-poor budget should be simply understood as a budget which reduces poverty as measured by an appropriate indicator. More precisely, a pro-poor budget is one where the income and/or opportunity of poor households after the budget's incidence is taken into account is greater than without it. Such a focus on impact highlights the fact that a political commitment to poverty alleviation is not enough. Nor, for that matter, are appropriately conceived and prioritised budget allocations. What matters is that the budget makes a discernible difference to measurable poverty indicators and the way poor households perceive their lived experience. Political commitment, economic stability and allocative efficiency are, of course, necessary conditions for a pro-poor impact. But to focus exclusively on these is to leave out of account a range of other equally significant factors that may determine the success of pro-poor budgeting.

3. Budget reforms and budgeting challenges

In many developing countries, particularly in the wake of the budgetary reforms of the 1990s,[10] fiscal policy has become more prudent and there has been a growing recognition of the need to prioritise services that target the poor. It has also been recognised that the budget system[11] must accurately identify social priorities, respond to them through policy development and a corresponding commitment of resources, and embody sufficient oversight capabilities to ensure that spending, taxation and borrowing match what has been proposed by the executive and approved by the legislature.

However, there have been many budgeting failures, and these persist. Macro-failures have included unrealistic estimates of growth and tax revenues; an inability or unwillingness to expand the tax base and a consequent over-reliance on external funding, both concessional and commercial; and loose monetary policies, even where there is a formal commitment to price stability.

In many developing countries, systemic budget challenges[12] have included weak control over departmental expenditure, particularly where accrual-based accounting systems have been adopted, and the opposite problem of underspending because departments suffer from severe capacity constraints. Budget systems have not always generated a set of allocations that reflects social priorities, and they may be skewed in favour of ministries with more political clout. A weak culture of accountability associated with weak legislatures and civil society, coupled with the absence of meaningful electoral competition, have perpetuated such problems. In many contexts, inadequate financial and non-financial budgeting information have made it more difficult to rationally draft and evaluate budgets, and the comparison of alternative means of attaining objectives on even a rough cost-benefit basis is almost impossible.[13] Taken together, these and similar challenges are likely to lead to a budget outcome that does not correspond sufficiently closely to the proposed budget. Typically, this also means that the budget's objectives in respect of poverty alleviation are not fulfilled.[14] From a governance perspective, a continuing divergence between what budgets propose and their outcomes erodes the confidence of stakeholders and reduces incentives for budgetary adherence in government departments.

Globally, attempts to reform budgeting to enhance its impact have led to experiments in "performance budgeting", which seeks to move from a procedural or "line item" orientation to one that is results-based and aims to meet certain objectives. Allocative and operational efficiencies are vital in determining whether a budget attains its objectives; they imply that for optimal budgetary performance, the right things need to be provided with a minimum of waste. The challenge of achieving allocative efficiency in a democracy is essentially one of ensuring that budget allocations mirror the preferences of voters.[15]

Operational efficiency relates firstly to the capacity of the state and secondly to whether performance incentives apply in public spending entities. Particularly in developing countries, where human capital may be a challenge, capacity implies that budget policy should match the scope for execution. Overly ambitious growth, employment or poverty initiatives that are not informed by an accurate sense of the financial, human and other resource constraints do far less for the poor than smaller-scale interventions that are implemented effectively. They not only have less impact; they further erode confidence in government.

A key requirement for operational efficiency is a meritocratic bureaucracy, defined primarily by a system of incentives for civil servants that rewards performance and censures under-performance. The literature that deals with the attributes of the "developmental state" offers a good analysis of bureaucracies and their relationship with broader society. Evans (1992) uses the notion of "embedded autonomy" to emphasise the ideal role of the state as a non-partisan, developmental actor that is, at the same time, sufficiently embedded in society to establish effective partnerships with other stakeholders and embody society's aspirations.

Given that state resources are limited, it is vital that oversight functions and interventions to improve budgeting are based on a proper assessment of whether disappointing performance is the result of allocative or operational inefficiency; whether operational inefficiency stems from failures of capacity or the incentive system; or whether exogenous factors are largely responsible. Where poverty, for example, remains intractable, governments are more likely to blame exogenous factors. Equally, departments are more likely to cite "capacity" as a reason for failures than the lack of appropriate performance incentives in their management systems. To some extent, this can be addressed by means of more stringent reporting requirements and by ensuring that governance debates are based on better information. But there is also a hermeneutic dimension, in the sense that conclusions will always be constrained by the "interpretive horizon" within which discussions take place. This makes it all the more important that legislatures function as a space for debate and decision-making where a broad range of perspectives are heard and considered.

4. BUDGET OWNERSHIP AND SOCIAL CAPITAL

In the context of the previous section's closing paragraph, any discussion of pro-poor budgeting should take into account the fact that an excessive emphasis on the more technical aspects of preparing and evaluating budgets can easily lead to a situation where budgeting remains the preserve of specialists and technocrats. Insulating budgeting decisions, such as those on the fiscal policy stance, from consideration by legislators can impede broader debates. The failure to "demystify" technical debates in a way that makes the trade-offs they embody explicit and amenable to democratic discussion can also discourage broader participation. Though many aspects of macro-economic management are technical and should remain the preserve of technocrats, debates on the fundamental macro-economic trade-off between the needs of the present and future generations, and how a budget interprets and embodies these, should not take place only among specialists or in finance ministries.[16]

The degree of trust and social "ownership" a budget commands can play a decisive role in its impact on well-being and the alleviation of poverty. One perspective through which such questions have been explored, and which is relevant in considering the budget from a pro-poor perspective, is that of social capital. Although the term can be defined in various ways, most definitions are rooted in efforts to conceptualise the economic and budgetary consequences of the degree of trust and cohesion in societies.[17] Some of the potential benefits of higher levels of social capital – that is, of greater trust, risk-sharing propensity and cooperation – include:

- lower business costs, as trust can compensate for information asymmetry in many contexts;
- better partnerships between the private and public sector, flowing from a broadly shared vision;
- more security, in the form of "safety nets" that supplement those provided publicly or commercially. This in turn facilitates more entrepreneurial risk-taking, including among the poor;
- less corrosive conflict over public resources and their allocation; and
- more emphasis on consensual decision-making and the maximum integration of all social partners in policy.

These benefits can generate a higher social multiplier effect and, all else being equal, a greater social return on the budget. There is also the possibility of a "virtuous circle" where social capital enhances budgeting and the budget in turn contributes to the development of social capital. Though such benefits are real and can be highly significant, this does not mean that they are easy to measure or, for that matter, that it is easy to enhance social capital. The determinants of a given stock of social capital are multi-dimensional and rooted as much in historical factors as in measures designed to address current needs.

Nevertheless, where social capital is high, it is more likely that trust and cooperation will also characterise the budget cycle of drafting, approval, implementation and evaluation. In such conditions, it is more likely that the budget will be allocatively efficient, since allocations are more likely to be determined in a participatory way and to match the priorities of the poor. They are also less likely to reflect asymmetries of power in society or government, leading to the more efficient setting of priorities. On the revenue side, tax compliance is also likely to be better in societies which share a common vision and where most citizens see the government as legitimate. Finally, in governance contexts where social capital is high, accountability is likely to be enhanced both because "ownership" entails scrutiny by all stakeholders, and because there is likely to be a more conducive environment for an objective and broad-ranging evaluation of what has worked and failed, and the best way forward.[18]

One of the main corroders of social capital is the perception that income distribution is unfair. For this reason, a redistributive fiscus that is perceived as fair by enough of the population can contribute significantly to creating a national environment where social capital can develop. Social capital also tends to be very low below a certain income threshold: very poor households have little time, energy or opportunity to maintain and build further relations of trust and cooperation. Thus, in addition to measures aimed at reducing inequality, the eradication of extreme poverty through targeted transfers and programmatic expenditure is likely to increase social connections in the beneficiary group, and the economic benefits associated with them.

The degree to which communities participate in fiscal decision-making can have a large impact on social capital formation and erosion, independently of the policies themselves. When citizens feel that they can influence how resources are generated and allocated – and this requires adequate levels of transparency, as well as formal participatory channels – they are more likely to engage in the robust debate and discussion, directly or through legislatures, that can create significant social capital. At present, South Africa enjoys a high level of transparency in its public finances, especially at national government level. However, citizens are not using the opportunities available through Parliament and the medium-term expenditure framework to engage with budget policy and the relevant economic data.[19]

Providing legislative space for debates about poverty and the impact of poverty measures is also important in establishing a "feedback loop" which informs the modification of existing programmes, as well as thinking about new initiatives and failed initiatives which need to be abandoned. More fundamentally, it is necessary to listen to those who live in poverty and have a grassroots perspective on their lives, to ensure that programmes are doing the right things. Also, providing a forum where talk can take place empowers the poor, as the sense of being voiceless is a key dimension of the qualitative experience of poverty.

5. Aspects of poverty in South Africa

Reducing the poverty of historically disadvantaged South Africans was a key objective of the ANC when it came to power and has remained a central policy priority. As success in attaining this is a key test of the government's performance to date, what can be asserted with reasonable certainty about trends in poverty rates from 1994 to 2008 and the extent to which government measures have influenced them?

Firstly, it is probable that income poverty was not significantly reduced between 1994 and about 2001. Using census 1996 and 2001 data, Leibrandt et al. (2006: 105) conclude that "measured poverty worsened between 1996 and 2001 at any poverty line". Their analysis also confirms the continued concentration of poverty among Africans, coloured people and Indians/Asians. As shown in table 1, using a poverty line of R250 per household per month (1996 rands) – higher than the $2 a day often used in inter-country comparisons – they compare trends in headcount poverty rates per population group.

Table 1: Trends in headcount poverty rates by population group, initial post-democratic phase		
	Headcount poverty rate (1996 Leibrandt)	Headcount poverty rate (2001 Leibrandt)
African	62%	67%
Coloured	34%	41%
Asian/Indian	11%	14%
White	3%	4%

However, the authors also point out that when improved access to basic services such as appropriate housing, water, energy, sanitation and telephones is taken into account, the picture becomes more complicated. "Even though income poverty seems to have increased, access to basic services has improved, suggesting increased well-being according to these measures" (2006: 131). Comparing changes in the percentage of income quintiles with access to these services in 1996 and in 2001, they conclude that "even though the poorest quintiles are most deprived, it is generally these households that are experiencing the greatest gains" (2006:131). The combined impact of fairly intractable income poverty in this period and improved and apparently well-targeted access to services is very difficult to determine. A further complication is that the access measure may itself be subject to a range of caveats regarding its impact on well-being. Although the evidence is not beyond dispute, there are grounds for thinking that many households recorded as being newly connected to services such as water and electricity would find it difficult to afford municipal service charges. So income poverty would, in fact, diminish the ability of households to actualise the gains in well-being associated with service availability.

The reasons for the fairly intractable rate of income poverty in the initial years of democracy are well established and documented. First and foremost, the South African economy did not grow particularly quickly in this period. Though it did grow more quickly than in the final years of apartheid, it certainly did not grow fast enough to have a significant effect on the unemployment rate and thus on the contribution of earned income to poverty reduction.

Public finance measures were in turn constrained by the impact of low growth on tax revenue; by the need to reduce the debt stock and attendant debt servicing burden; and by the limited absorptive capacity of many departments in the initial bureaucratic transition period.[20] Though there was a significant budgetary reallocation of basic and social services towards the historically disadvantaged,[21] the total resource envelope in which this occurred remained constrained. Furthermore, the ability of national and provincial departments to spend efficiently was itself a function of income. Quite often, it was administrations in the poorer provinces that struggled to deliver poverty-related services.

However, both Bhorat (2008) and Van der Berg (2007) find a significant decline in the headcount rate of poverty and the depth and severity of poverty in the subsequent period.[22] Table 2 compares their findings. (Differences in percentage values result from the use of different poverty lines).

Table 2: Recent poverty trends: headcount income poverty		1993	1995	2000	2004	2005	2006
Van der Berg							
	All	50.1	51.7	50.8	46.9		44.4
	Black	63.0	64.7	62.3	57.0		
Bhorat (R322 per month)							
	All		52.5			48.0	
	Black		63.0			56.3	
Bhorat (R174 per month)							
	All		30.9			22.7	
	Black		38.2			27.2	

Regarding the depth of poverty – the average gap between the poverty line and the income of those falling below it – both authors also find significant improvements in the post-2001 period.[23]

There is a strong consensus that a key factor in improved income poverty rates has been the extension of social grants. Indeed, Van der Berg provides three related reasons for these trends: the expansion of grants; the possibility of higher wages or increased employment, suggested by a real remuneration increase of R100-billion between 2002 and 2006 in the national accounts data; and the fact that income distribution among black people is clustered fairly closely around the poverty lines used in his study, implying that a small shift in income distribution would have a potentially large impact on the measured poverty rate (Van der Berg et al., 2007: 22).

Stats SA's 2005/06 income and expenditure survey(IES)also indicates that between 2000 and 2005/06, mean real per capita income increased for all ten income deciles. The relevant table from the survey is reproduced below:

Table 3: Changes in real per capita income per decile, IES 2000 to IES 2005/06											
Income decile	1	2	3	4	5	6	7	8	9	10	Average
% change IES 2000 to IES 2005/06	79	41	36	31	29	26	28	25	26	37	33

The table suggests that income increased by a greater than average amount for deciles 1, 2, 3 and 10, that is, the poorest three and the richest, with the most pronounced improvement in the poorest. The higher than average increase in income in the three poorest deciles most probably reflects the impact of means-tested social grants, as households in these deciles are unlikely to have many members in regular employment.

Social grants have been one of the fastest-growing items of budget expenditure since 2001 and the number of beneficiaries increased to close to 13-million in 2008, as take-up rates improved and eligibility criteria were adjusted upwards.[24] South Africa spends slightly more than three percent of GDP on such direct income transfers. Recent research (Delany, A et al., 2008 and De Koker, C. et al. 2006) has found that grants largely benefit poor households and considerably enhance the well-being of households that receive them. Delany et al. found fairly low rates of erroneous inclusion and exclusion, that is, cases where ineligible households received grants and eligible households did not. The study also found clear differences between the circumstances of children in households that received grants and those in poor households that did not.

However, concerns have been raised about the level of fiscal risk associated with further expansion beyond the intended increases in age-eligibility for the child support grant and the state pension.[25] Means-tested direct income transfers, like other forms of entitlement spending, can generate a great deal of fiscal pressure in adverse circumstances, as they are more difficult to scale down than they are to expand. These concerns are given greater relevance by the contraction of the global economy and its impact on South Africa at the time of writing. The contraction means that the radical expansion of social grants as a tool in the fight against poverty is unlikely.

Despite the real gains that have been made, South Africa remains a country where at least half of the population lives with some form of "capability deprivation" associated with inadequate access to income, assets and opportunity. A recent study of poverty that used the socially perceived necessities approach makes it clear that a large percentage of black, coloured and Indian people remain deprived of many essentials needed for a decent life[26] (Wright, G., 2008). The study asked respondents to list the essentials for a decent life and to evaluate their circumstances in terms of their access to them. It found that "there is a discrepancy between the standard of living which people regard as acceptable and the standard of living that is currently experienced by many people in South Africa" (Wright 2008: 9). More specifically, the study found that large percentages of households in South Africa lack many of the goods and services they regard as essential.

6. SOME BUDGET CHALLENGES IN DEMOCRATIC SOUTH AFRICA

Not surprisingly, given the social and economic challenges and the state of public finances in 1994, there has at times been fierce controversy over democratic South Africa's budget policy. Much of the acrimony between the ANC and its alliance partners, Cosatu and the SACP, stems from the introduction of the Growth, Employment and Redistribution (Gear) programme in 1996. Tensions were sparked by the contents of Gear and the lack of consultation in drawing up the policy, as well as its presentation as "non-negotiable". Cosatu and the SACP saw the policy as being excessively austere in its commitment to reducing budget deficits, and as too readily adopting the fundamental assumptions of the "Washington Consensus", with its neo-liberal emphasis.

Though tensions over economic and budget policy persist in the alliance, and these played a part in the ousting of Thabo Mbeki as ANC president at the ANC's national conference in Polokwane in 2007, budget policy since about 2001 has become considerably more expansionary. Following significant real increases in non-interest expenditure in this period, often in excess of the economic growth rate, the government's share of GDP slowly climbed to just under 30 percent in the 2009/10 budget, from the low twenties.

Budget debates on the fiscal policy stance and issues of allocative efficiency continue, as they must, and include questions such as the appropriateness of budget surpluses in some recent budgets, the feasibility of further expanding social grants, greater capitalisation by the fiscus of state-owned enterprises and a more assertively funded industrial policy. In general, however, most commentators would endorse the allocative dimension of recent budgets, with their prioritisation of social spending, particularly education spending; the significant roll-out of basic household services to historically excluded areas; attempts to constrain recurrent expenditure and increase government and public sector gross fixed capital formation; and the coverage of grants, which at more than three percent of GDP is high by global standards. It is probably fair to say that debates about allocative efficiency currently focus on which initiatives should be expanded at the margin, rather than on the broad allocative efficiency of the budget as such.

The medium-term expenditure framework (MTEF) has also succeeded in establishing a budget process that a range of stakeholders finds credible and predictable and that gives government departments a sense of the parameters in which they must frame their budget bids. The MTEF has forced departments and other spending entities to conceive of their operations and financing requirements over a longer period than merely the coming year, bringing greater stability to budgeting and substantially reducing *ad hoc* adjustments and tinkering. It is generally recognised that the South African budget system is also characterised by a high degree of transparency,[27] certainly at national level and in varying degrees at provincial level. This facilitates formal participation by interest groups and gives legislatures useful information in fulfilling their oversight roles.[28] The Medium-Term Budget Policy Statement (MTBPS), for example, tells interested groups well in advance what, in broad terms, the next budget and the two subsequent budgets will look like. Idasa has argued, in fact, that neither civil society nor Parliament has done enough to take advantage of the opportunities provided by high budget transparency, particularly the MTBPS.[29]

The MTBPS outlines significant sectoral shifts and the government's assumptions on the medium-term direction of the economy, but does not provide indicative allocations disaggregated by vote, which somewhat reduces its value. The Money Bills Amendment Act, discussed in detail in subsequent chapters, requires the executive to give more information on specific allocations in the MTBPS. This increases the administrative burden on the executive, but should facilitate a more detailed engagement with the budget in February and, crucially, in the months before it is tabled. [30]

In democratic South Africa, budget reforms have also included a shift to performance budgeting. The Public Finance Management Act, which covers national and provincial departments and other spending entities, and the Municipal Finance Management Act, which does the same for local government, articulate this emphasis on performance and the related dimension of framing departmental operations in terms of measurable objectives. The National Treasury has also released guidelines to assist departments in planning, budgeting, implementing and evaluating themselves from a performance perspective. [31] It is probably fair to say, however, that the shift to performance budgeting in departments, and the ability of legislatures to oversee performance, remains a work in progress. For example, the Auditor-General does not conduct performance audits to the same extent as financial audits, and a recent report by this office highlights the uncertain legal status of the National Treasury's programme framework for performance information (Auditor General of South Africa 2009: 11).

Broad fiscal policy has consolidated public finances and facilitated significant real increases in public spending since 2001, and the budget process is largely credible and generates a generally appropriate mix of public goods and services. So what acute challenges remain in the field of poverty alleviation, which should form a key aspect of legislative engagement in the years ahead?

It is fair to say that the challenges South Africa faces relate less to fiscal sustainability and allocative efficiency than to operational efficiency – the translation of allocations into outputs and outcomes that have the desired impact, meeting the measurable objectives for which money was allocated in the first place. There is evidence of operational inefficiency both in the disappointing impact of key social departments and in some of the available information on the quality of financial management in departments.

Despite the large sums of money allocated to education, both absolutely and relative to total spending, South Africa's education system struggles to provide the skills required by the economy, and perhaps particularly by sectors with higher growth potential, such as export-orientated manufacturing. At the end of 2008, matric pass rates fell again to just 62.7 percent, with almost 200 000 pupils failing the exam. The national and provincial education ministries also underperformed: more than 56 000 pupils did not get their results because of technical glitches and provinces not handing in their class marks (Department of Education 2008). These statistics underscore the continued poor performance of teachers and administrators. In his 2009 budget speech, former finance minister Trevor Manuel also highlighted the systemic inefficiency of the education system as an area of ongoing concern.

The 2008 matric pass rates are not surprising if one considers the poor perform-ance of South African learners at lower levels of schooling. The education depart-ment's own evaluations of the performance of learners in grade 3, in 2001, and grade 6, in 2004, highlighted the problems. Grade 3 learners averaged 68 percent for listening comprehension, but only 39 percent for reading comprehension and writing, 30 percent for numeracy and 54 percent for life skills. Grade 6 learners averaged 38 percent for language, 27 percent for mathematics and 41 percent in the natural sciences.

Furthermore, South African learners continue to perform poorly in standardised international assessments of maths and science ability. They have scored consistently poorly in the Trends in International Mathematics and Science Study, which meas-ures the maths and science achievements of eighth-graders. South African learners scored an average of 275 in maths and 243 in science in the inaugural study in 1999, placing them at the bottom of the 38 nations surveyed. The highest-scoring group of learners, from Singapore and China Taipei, scored 604 and 569 for maths and science respectively (NCED 1999). In the 2003 assessment South African learners fared no better, again finishing last in both categories and lagging far behind other African countries such as Ghana and Botswana. Even more worrying was the fact that between 1999 and 2003, the average score dropped by 11 points in mathemat-ics and only increased by one point in science (NCED 2003). In other words, South Africa not only scores poorly in an absolute sense in such surveys, but also scores more poorly than one would expect, given its per capita income and available public resources. Considering the funds allocated to education in a fairly large budget by the standards of developing countries, it becomes even clearer that institutional perform-ance is a major problem. As already noted, a key challenge of legislative oversight is determining the extent to which lack of technical expertise ("capacity") or inad-equate performance incentives account for these failures.

The public health sector is also beset with challenges of operational efficiency. The issue seems less one of access to healthcare than access to quality healthcare, espe-cially at the public hospitals which most South Africans use. Most tellingly perhaps, the majority of citizens continue to regard publicly provided healthcare as an inferior good – one for which demand varies inversely with income. Even comparatively poor and uninsured households appear to strive to gain access to private healthcare, be-lieving that they will receive better clinical care and personal treatment.[32]

Recent annual reports of the health department show under-expenditure in each of its four programmes – administration, strategic health programmes, health service delivery and human resources. The under-spending points to difficulties in reach-ing optimal operational efficiency. Problems with the workforce have stymied the goal of adequate service delivery. The intractability of this problem is indicated by the absence of an effective education and skills training programme for healthcare professionals that ensures that patients using public hospitals receive adequate care. The Health Systems Trust's 2008 *South African Health Review* found that "overall the health workforce is substantially weaker than it was in the mid-1990s" (Health Systems Trust 2008:163). In addition, the gap between private and public healthcare has grown since that time. Inefficiency and lack of capacity at provincial level has also led to disparities in treatment. According to Health Systems Trust, the nursing sector faces a "serious crisis brought on by an aging professional population" (2008:163). Recent work on the underperformance of public hospitals also suggests that some of the challenges facing South African public hospitals are rooted in a complex set of tensions that are not easily susceptible to simple financial, managerial or political intervention (Von Holdt, forthcoming). However complex the problems, hand-wringing is not an adequate response. As in the case of education, legislative oversight is crucial to understanding these challenges, finding workable solutions and ensuring that proposed measures are properly implemented and evaluated.

While financial management is merely one dimension of operational efficiency, it says a great deal about the capacity of staff and the quality of systems. Institutions that receive an adverse opinion or disclaimer from the Auditor-General are unlikely to provide efficient and effective services.[33] A cursory glance at expenditure by government departments across a fiscal year, for example, shows a strong tendency for many departments to spend excessively in the fourth quarter.[34] "Fiscal dumping" need not point to inefficiency and ineffectiveness, but it suggests that key social departments tend to spend allocated funds mainly to look good on paper, avoid censure and ensure that the department is not disadvantaged in future budget-bidding, rather than because of a commitment to service delivery.

The Auditor-General's reports on the financial management of departments have also suggested that many departments still struggle to account for allocations in line with sound financial management principles and the requirements of the Public Finance Management Act and Municipal Finance Management Act. Briefing Parliament on the audit outcomes for 2007/08, for example, the Auditor-General reported that only 23 percent of the 463 audited national and provincial departments, institutions and entities had received an unqualified ("clean") financial opinion.

The shortage of clean audit opinions suggests that much work remains to be done; it does not imply that government is riddled with gross mismanagement and corruption. Of the qualified audit opinions given to these entities, a comparatively small percentage suggested serious financial management failures. Two percent were "adverse"; five percent contained disclaimers; 23 percent were financially qualified; and 47 percent were unqualified opinions that raised concerns about "other matters", mainly internal controls, governance arrangements and legislative compliance. Twenty-three percent were unqualified, with no other concerns being recorded in the audit opinion.

The "other matters" recorded show that 44 percent of national and provincial departments did not comply fully with the Public Finance Management Act's requirements. (Auditor-General of South Africa 2009: 3). Audits picked up material amendments to the financial statements in 59 percent of departments, suggesting that their controls and monitoring were inadequate.

The Auditor-General's 2006/07 report on local government reveals an even more challenging situation. In that financial year, a distressing 53 percent of municipalities received an adverse opinion or disclaimer. A further 26 percent received qualified financial opinions; 20 percent were financially unqualified but with other matters raised, and only one percent – a total of three municipalities – received a "clean" audit opinion.

Figure 1 below shows the concentration of municipalities that received adverse audit opinions or disclaimers in 2006/07, by province.

Figure 1: 2006/07 adverse opinions and disclaimers for municipalities, by province

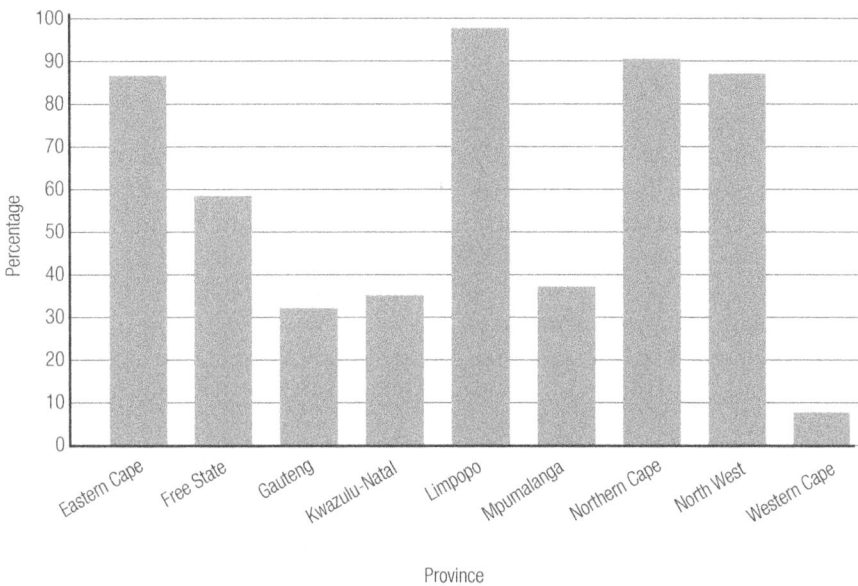

Institutional failures, such as those discussed in the health and education sectors, together with problems in financial management, suggest that issues of operational efficiency remain the main obstacle to maximising the budget's impact on poverty. Such failures may stem from a lack of capacity or appropriate performance incentives, or both, or may be the result of factors exogenous to the performance of departments. From the perspective of oversight by legislatures and other stakeholders, it is crucial that the reasons for performance failures are clearly determined, supported by available evidence.

"Lack of capacity" is too often used in South African governance debates to account for performance failures. A Parliament keen on exercising effective oversight should not accept it so readily, and should ensure that departments are taking concrete steps to address their alleged capacity problems. Departments should also be required to identify whether the capacity problems they refer to stem from high vacancy rates at more senior levels, from a poor alignment of the required and available skills, from failures of departmental coordination, or from other matters. Oversight committees should also try to assess the extent to which exogenous factors may be fuelling capacity problems. Two obvious instances are where departments face such an onerous regulatory and broader compliance burden that they find it difficult to get anything done, and where they are not given sufficient resources to do the work expected of them.

8. CONCLUSION: SOME COMMENTS ON PARLIAMENTARY OVERSIGHT

Effective oversight of performance rests on a number of conditions. One of these is adequate transparency: the timely availability of comprehensive and accessible information on allocations, spending and, as far as possible, delivery of services. However, this is not enough. To work effectively, legislative oversight committees must have access to departments' strategic plans, information on allocations by programme and sub-programme, in-year spending reports, annual reports and Auditor-General's reports. Also required is the political will to ensure accountability and legislative research capacity to support committees.

Through the Public Finance Management Act, South Africa has made significant strides in giving legislatures the formal oversight authority to ensure that government departments conceive and report on their operations in terms of measurable objectives linked to budget allocations, so that value for money can be assessed. In-year spending reports and Auditor-General's reports are also readily available. Although executive-legislative relations are always marked by information symmetry, effective oversight of budgetary performance does not require that legislatures know as much as departmental accounting officers about what departments are doing and the impact of their work. It is not necessary to eliminate all information asymmetries for genuine oversight to take place. What is required is that committees can ask the right questions when they summon accounting officers, and that they continue to probe until they feel satisfied that they have an adequate sense of a department's performance. The documents currently available to committees are a sufficient basis for the right questions. The onus must always be on the executive to satisfy a committee that its planning and spending is efficient in allocative and operational terms.

If significant uncertainty persists about a department's performance, a committee could recommend the provisional withholding of increased allocations until doubts have been cleared up to its satisfaction. The department in question could supply further information to show that its performance has been satisfactory, or acknowledge that its performance has been disappointing. Before increased allocations are considered, it would then have to satisfy the committee that it is taking concrete, significant and realistic steps to remedy the shortcomings. Crucially, the committee should follow up on the agreed remedial steps, checking that the department is according them the necessary priority. Without such follow-up scrutiny, oversight risks becoming something of a sham that meets formal governance requirements but has little chance of improving the impact of spending on poverty alleviation.

Effective oversight also means that legislatures and stakeholders engaged in budget work, such as non-governmental organisations, should get to grips with the medium-term orientation of the MTEF and keep abreast of policy and shifts in allocations over this time-frame. Only from such a perspective is it possible to get a sense of the performance of departments and assess their plans in an informed way. Too often, civil society and legislatures restrict their budgetary engagement to last-minute responses to documents tabled in February, relegating themselves to irrelevance.

As discussed in detail in chapter four, a well-resourced and independent budget research office can give invaluable support to legislatures in this area, and it is imperative that the office has adequate capacity and tailors its research work to medium-term strategic priorities.

Finally, legislatures must see that facilitating participation in budget oversight is a key dimension of their work. Civil society organisations can bring valuable perspectives not only to the consideration of the budget as a whole, but also on specific sectoral issues. Such participation, in conjunction with a budget research office, can do much to close the capacity gap between the executive and the legislature in budgeting matters. But participation is important not only for oversight; it also fosters greater "ownership" of the budget. The intentions of a budget are most likely to be realised when it is seen as articulating a vision shared by the government and citizens. It will then activate citizens' aspirations, in a way that is unlikely to happen if it is conceived in isolation by ministers and officials.

REFERENCES

Ajam, T. and J. Aron, "Fiscal Renaissance in a Democratic South Africa", *Journal of African Economies* Volume 16, Issue 5, 2007.

Auditor General of South Africa, 2009 *General Report on the Audit Outcomes for the Departments, Constitutional Institutions, Public Entities and other Entities for the Financial Year* 2007/08, available at: www.agsa.co.za
– *General Report on the Audit Outcomes of Local Government for Financial Year* 2006/07, available at www.agsa.co.za

Bhorat, H. and R. Kanbur, "Introduction: Poverty and Well-Being in Post-Apartheid South Africa" in *Poverty and Policy in Post-Apartheid South Africa* Bhorat, H. and R. Kanbur (eds.) Human Sciences Research Council: Cape Town, 2006.

Bhorat, H. and C. Van der Westhuizen, "Economic Growth, Poverty and Inequality in South Africa: The First Decade of Democracy". Paper commissioned for the Presidency's *Towards a 15-Year Review*, 2008.

Buchanan, J. and G. Tullock, *The Calculus of Consent*, Ann Arbor Michigan: University of Michigan Press, 1962.

Centre for Budget and Policy Priorities, *Open Budget Index 2009*, available at www.internationalbudget.org

Claassens, M. and A. Van Zyl, (eds.), *Budget Transparency and Participation 2, Nine African Case Studies*, Idasa, Cape Town, 2005.

De Koker, C., L. de Waal and J. Vorster, *A Profile of Social Security Beneficiaries in South Africa, Volume 1* and *Volume 2*, University of Stellenbosch, 2006.

Delany, A., Z. Ismail, L. Graham and Y. Ramkissoon, *Review of the Child Support Grant: Uses, Implementation and Obstacles*. Report compiled by CASE for the Department of Social Development and Unicef, 2008.

Department of Education, *National Senior Certificate Results 2008*, Presentation to the Portfolio Committee on Education, 2009.

Evans, P., "The State as Problem and Solution: Predation, Embedded Autonomy and Structural Change", in *The Politics of Economic Adjustment*, Haggard, S. and R. Kaufman (eds.), Princeton: Princeton, New Jersey, 1992.

Faulkner, D. and C. Loewald, "Policy Change and Economic Growth: A Case Study of South Africa", Commission on Growth and Development: Working Paper No. 41, available at: www.growthcommission.org, 2008.

Health Systems Trust, *South African Health Review* 2008, available at www.hst.org.za

Idasa, "Budget 2009: Still Getting the Balance Right?", PIMS Budget Paper 4, available at www.idasa.org, 2009.
– "Trends in 2006/07 Departmental Expenditure: Submission to the Joint Budget Committee", 2006.
– "MTBPS 2006: Parliament, ASGISA and Infrastructure", available at: www.idasa.org, 2006.

Kanbur, R. and L. Squire, "The Evolution of Thinking about Poverty: Exploring the Interactions", available at: www.unstats.un.org, 1999.

Leibrandt, M., L. Poswell, P. Naidoo, and M. Welch, "Measuring Recent Changes in South African Inequality and Poverty using 1996 and 2001 Census Data", in *Poverty and Policy in Post-Apartheid South Africa*, Bhorat, H. and R. Kanbur, (eds.), Human Sciences Research Council: Cape Town, 2006.

National Treasury, *Framework for Managing Programme Performance Information*, available at: www.finance.gov.za, 2007.

National Center for Education Statistics, *Trends in International Mathematics and Science Study*, 1999, available at www.nces.ed.gov

National Center for Education Statistics, *Trends in International Mathematics and Science Study*, 2003, available at www.nces.ed.gov

Pauw, K. and L. Mncube, "Expanding the Social Security Net in South Africa: Opportunities, Challenges and Constraints", International Poverty Centre Country Study Number 8, 2007.

Quist, R., C. Certan and J. Dendura, "Republic of South Africa: Public Expenditure and Financial Accountability", available at: www.finance.gov.za, 2008.

Rodrik, D., "Democracy and Economic Performance", Paper prepared for a Conference on Democratization and Economic Reform in South Africa, Cape Town 1998.

Sen, A., *Development as Freedom*, Oxford University Press: Oxford, 1999.

Stats SA, "Income and Expenditure of Households 2005/2006: Analysis of Results", available at: www.statssa.gov.za, 2007.

– "Measuring Poverty in South Africa", available at www.statssa.gov.za, 2000.

South African Government, "Towards an Anti-Poverty Strategy for South Africa: A Discussion Document", available at: www.info.gov.za, 2008.

Van der Berg, S., M. Louw and L. du Toit, "Poverty Trends Since the Transition: What We Know", Department of Economics, Stellenbosch University, 2007.

Van der Berg, S., "Fiscal Expenditure Incidence in South Africa: A Report for the National Treasury", available at: www.sarpn.org.za, 2005.

Von Holdt, K., "The South African Post-Apartheid Bureaucracy: Inner Workings, Contradictory Rationales and the Developmental State", in *Constructing a Democratic Developmental State in South Africa: Potential and Challenges*; edited by Edigheji, O, HSRC Press, Forthcoming.

Walker, L. and B. Mengistu, *Spend & Deliver: The Medium-Term Expenditure Framework*, Idasa: Cape Town, 1999.

Wright, G., *A Profile of Poverty Using the Socially Perceived Necessities Approach*, Indicators of Poverty and Social Exclusion Project, Centre for the Analysis of South African Social Policy, Commissioned by the Department of Social Development, 2008.

Chapter 2

South Africa's new parliamentary budget process:
an initial assessment

Joachim Wehner

1. INTRODUCTION

In the wake of its transition to democracy, South Africa had an opportunity to reshape the role of its legislatures in a fundamental way. The apartheid-era Parliaments had been feeble and discredited rubber stamps (Kotzé 1996). In contrast, the country's new constitutional framework promised "dynamic and pro-active legislatures" (Murray and Nijzink 2002: 1). The first democratic Parliament abolished apartheid-era legislation and processed the fast-evolving public policy agenda of the new government (Calland 1999). At the same time, Parliament itself was undergoing organisational change, including the creation of a system of legislative committees (Calland 1997) and the implementation of a new bicameral structure (Murray and Simeon 1999).

One of the issues to be reconsidered by the democratic Parliament was its role in the budgetary process. Section 77 of the 1996 Constitution gave Parliament the power to amend money bills, but required enabling legislation to regulate the process. In the absence of this legislation, parliamentarians could only approve or reject budgets in their entirety, and they made not one amendment to money bills in more than a decade of democracy.[35] There were two legislative initiatives to address the constitutional requirement of regulation of the amendment process, as well as a number of abortive attempts that never made it into the public domain. In this chapter, I provide a comparative overview of legislative budget institutions and assess the two major reform attempts – the 1997 draft Money Bills Amendment Procedure Bill and the 2009 Money Bills Amendment Procedure and Related Matters Act. In the conclusion, I consider to what extent the adopted framework facilitates an active parliamentary process while safeguarding fiscal prudence.

2. LEGISLATIVE BUDGETING IN COMPARATIVE PERSPECTIVE

Two sets of literature provide useful frameworks for assessing the design of the legislative budget process in South Africa and possible options for its reform. The first is the literature on comparative legislatures, which in recent years has developed a more systematic approach to the study of cross-national differences. The second is the political economy literature on the common pool resource problem in budgeting, which discusses specific institutional features of the legislative process and how they affect fiscal performance. In this section, I provide a brief overview of these.

There is a long tradition of mostly qualitative literature comprising case studies of legislative budgeting in a number of countries (for example, Coombes 1976, Oppenheimer 1983, Schick 2002). However, until very recently, there was no systematic comparison of the budgetary role of legislatures across a wider spread of countries.

Partly, this was due to a lack of data. However, over the past ten years the Organisation for Economic Cooperation and Development (OECD) has conducted a number of surveys of budget institutions, which also cover the legislative phase of the budget process. Wehner (2006) uses the 2003 Survey of Budget Practices and Procedures, conducted by the OECD in co-operation with the World Bank, to carry out a comparative assessment of "the power of the purse" (see also Lienert 2005).

Legislative budget capacity can be conceptualised in different ways (Meyers 2001). Wehner (2006) adopts an institutional perspective and surveys six key variables that affect legislative control of the budget process: amendment powers; reversionary budget provisions; executive flexibility during implementation; the timing of the budget; committee capacity; and legislative budget research capacity. Figure 1 on the following page summarises the resulting ranking of 36 countries (for full details, see Wehner 2006). Possible scores on the index range between zero (no legislative budget capacity) and 100 (full capacity). Of the 36 countries included in the analysis, South Africa's Parliament obtained the lowest score, tied with the Irish Parliament. The scoring reflects the lack of amendment powers in the absence of constitutionally required enabling legislation; reversionary provisions that in practice allow the implementation of the government's proposal when budget approval is delayed; substantial executive flexibility to divert from the approved budget during its execution; the late tabling of the budget shortly before the start of the fiscal year; and the absence of a legislative budget office.[36] This analysis classified the South African Parliament as exceptionally weak in terms of its capacity for financial scrutiny.

Authors such as Stourm (1917) and Einzig (1959) bemoan the decline of Parliaments, but a second set of literature suggests that weak legislatures may be beneficial in terms of fiscal performance. Theoretical work on the common pool resource problem in budgeting highlights the fact that a proliferation of budgetary decision-makers gives rise to fiscal indiscipline (Weingast et al. 1981, Von Hagen and Harden 1995, Velasco 2000). However, institutional arrangements can mitigate "fiscal illusion" by vesting strategic power in actors who are likely to internalise costs, such as the finance minister (Von Hagen and Harden 1995). There is strong empirical support for this hypothesis, with evidence from Western Europe (Von Hagen 1992, Hallerberg et al. 2007), Latin America (Alesina et al. 1999, Filc and Scartascini 2004) and Central and Eastern Europe (Yläoutinen 2004, Fabrizio and Mody 2006), as well as a global sample of countries (Wehner 2008).

While the legislative arena can foster special interest claims on the budget, empirical studies suggest that certain institutional devices help to contain fiscal illusion in parliamentary decisions. Notably, several empirical studies conclude that limitations on legislative powers to amend the budget help to safeguard fiscal discipline (for example, Hallerberg and Marier 2004, Wehner 2008). In addition, another institutionalist hypothesis is that the size of budgets is influenced by the way the voting process is sequenced. Von Hagen (1992) initially suggested that fiscal discipline is enhanced when a vote on aggregate spending precedes decisions on allocation. However, this is contradicted by the work of Ferejohn and Krehbiel (1987), who

Figure 1: The index of legislative budget institutions (2003)

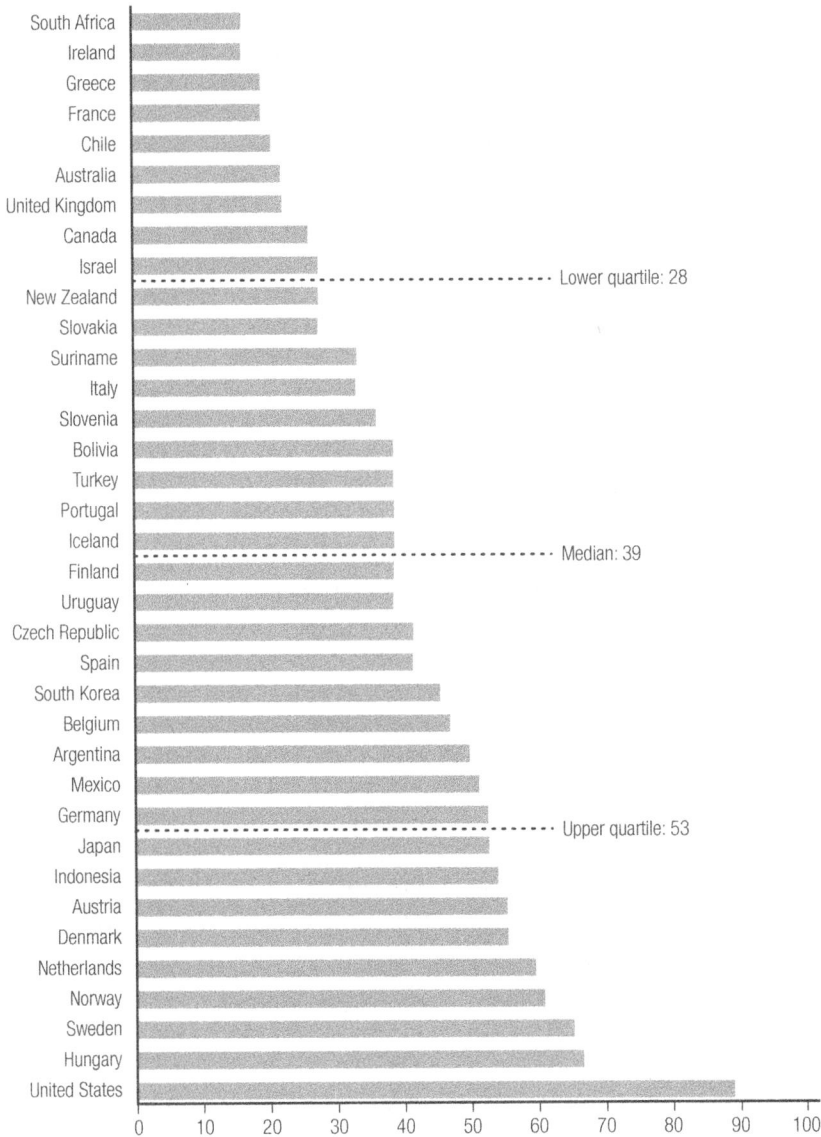

Source: Wehner (2006).

show that this process can produce relatively large budgets. Von Hagen later revised his initial claim, arguing that it is not the reordering of the voting sequence that is decisive, as it has no impact on the share of the tax burden that actors consider, but rather the centralisation of decision-making (Hallerberg and Von Hagen 1997; see also Ehrhart et al. 2007).

The fiscal benefit of the two-step process depends crucially on who makes the first decision on aggregates. If this decision is delegated to a group of actors who internalise a larger share of the costs than those with strong sectoral interests, fiscal discipline will be strengthened. However, as Perotti and Kontopoulos (2002: 196) summarise: "If the same agents decide at both stages, by backward induction they will take into account the likely allocations in the second stage when setting the total budget first." Hence, the delegation of the aggregate decision to a finance or budget committee, which can impose a hard budget constraint on various sectoral committees, should help to contain overall spending. As Crain and Muris (1995: 319) argue: "Consolidating control within one committee is an institutional means to overcome the common pool problem; it establishes a mechanism to contain spending pressures." On the other hand, with a balkanised committee setting, where partial spending decisions are distributed across a number of different committees, no one committee is responsible for the overall level of expenditure, which encourages free-riding.

Figure 2 presents stylised versions of three main types of committee structure for budget approval (Wehner 2007, see also Breton 1996: 105). In what I call the "dispersed" model, depicted on the left hand side of Figure 2, the different sectoral committees (labelled SC) make separate spending decisions on the parts of the budget that fall within their jurisdiction, such as health, education or defence. In the absence of binding constraints, such as hard expenditure ceilings or limitations on parliamentary amendment powers, the work by Crain and Muris (1995) suggests that this dispersed committee structure engenders a pro-spending bias. Figure 2 also illustrates two alternative approaches. The "hierarchical" model imposes a finance committee (labelled FC) with the power to determine a total expenditure ceiling as well as sectoral sub-ceilings that are binding for the sectoral committees. The latter consider allocations within their respective sector, but they have to adhere to the relevant sectoral ceiling established by the finance committee. A second alternative is the "exclusive" model, in which a finance committee is the sole budgetary decision-maker and sectoral committees are excluded from the process. The latter two models introduce centralisation and, therefore, would be expected to contain the common pool resource problem in the legislative arena.

Figure 2: Three models of committee structures for budgetary decisions

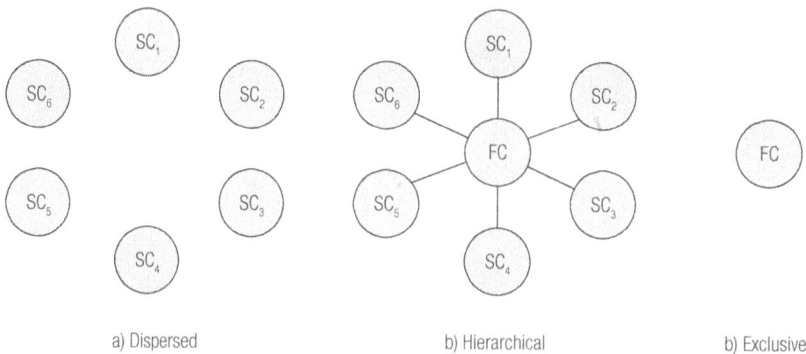

a) Dispersed   b) Hierarchical   b) Exclusive

Source: Wehner (2007). SC = sectoral committee; FC = finance committee

In summary, the literature points to a possible trade-off between legislative participation and prudent fiscal management. For more than a decade after the end of apartheid, the South African Parliament had an exceptionally weak role in the budget process. This helped to ensure executive control over fiscal policy, but also prevented substantive parliamentary involvement. The political economy literature on budgeting cautions that the common pool resource problem in legislatures is potentially large and gives rise to a pro-spending bias. Related work on the design of the budget process suggests that institutional devices can help to protect fiscal discipline, notably limitations on legislative powers to amend the budget and a top-down voting process in conjunction with a strong role for a finance or budget committee in aggregate decisions. In the following sections, I discuss the two main attempts to reform the parliamentary budget process in South Africa, and evaluate to what extent the latest effort is likely to strengthen Parliament's role and affect fiscal policy outcomes.

3. A FAILED FIRST ATTEMPT

With the appointment of Trevor Manuel as Minister of Finance in April 1996, South Africa embarked on an extensive programme of budget reform. There were multiple pressures for reform. On the one hand, the government had an ambitious service delivery agenda, but it also had to reassure the business community and to re-establish fiscal credibility to enhance foreign investment (Department of Finance 1996; for critical perspectives, see Michie and Padayachee 1998, Weeks 1999, Streak 2004). Before the 1994 elections, the consolidated general government deficit had deteriorated to nine percent of GDP, and the budget remained markedly unbalanced in the first few years of democracy (see Figure 3 on the following page). Budget reform had the potential to reconcile the demands for service delivery with fiscal consolidation.

Among the reforms was the implementation of a new system of inter-governmental fiscal relations in 1997, based on the Constitution's three-sphere structure of the national government, nine provincial governments and local authorities (Abedian et al. 1997). Also, in December 1997, the then Department of Finance published the first medium-term budget policy statement (MTBPS), a pre-budget report containing the policy framework for the upcoming budget and the two following "outer" years (Department of Finance 1997). The introduction of a medium-term framework enhanced the capacity of the finance minister to ensure reprioritisation, initially away from defence and towards social expenditure, within strict aggregate limits on spending (Walker and Mengistu 1999). These and other reforms earned South Africa praise from the International Monetary Fund (2003: 18), which commended the country for its "impressive track record in budgetary management".

The new constitutional framework demanded a range of changes to the budget process and included several specific requirements for legislation (Walker and Mengistu 1999: 48). Among these was the requirement in section 77(2) of the Constitution that "an Act of Parliament must provide for a procedure to amend money Bills before Parliament". Section 77(1) defined a money bill as a bill that "appropriates money or imposes taxes, levies or duties". A constitutional amendment in 2001 added further detail to this definition, but left the demand for legislation on an amendment procedure in place, now in section 77(3) of the Constitution. Both versions of the constitutional text are reproduced in Appendix 1 of this book.

Figure 3: Consolidated general government receipts and payments

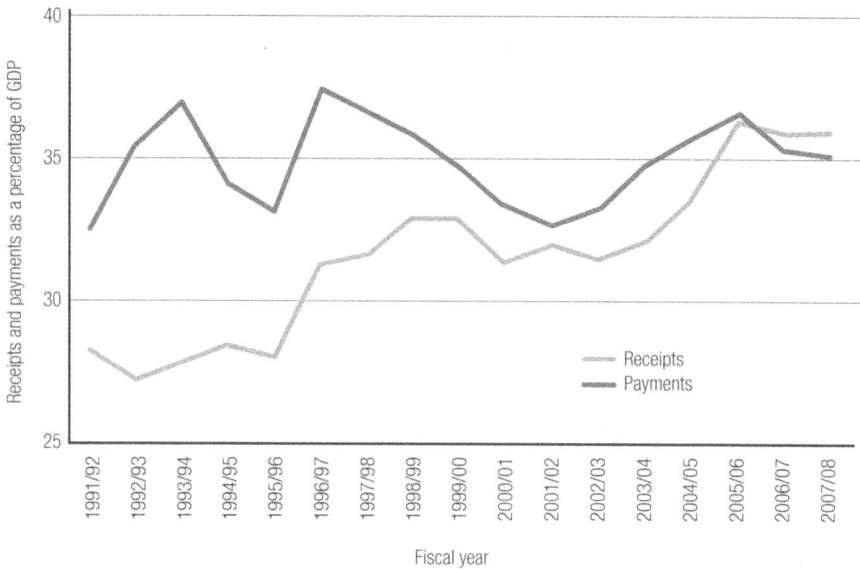

In a first attempt to address the constitutional demand for regulation of the parliamentary budget process, the Department of Finance produced a draft Money Bills Amendment Procedure Bill, which it prepared for tabling in Parliament in late 1997. The memorandum attached to the draft bill reveals the attitude that prevailed in the executive at the time. In dramatic language, it emphasised the need to "maintain the integrity of the budget and the tax system" and argued that the right to amend money bills "cannot be an unfettered right" so that "government is not paralysed in the process". This wording of the memorandum reflects the emphasis on fiscal consolidation that marked the early years of Manuel's tenure as finance minister. The executive perceived Parliament as a potential fiscal threat.

The draft bill reflected this attitude. The crucial provisions in part one (section 4) would have severely curtailed Parliament's powers to amend. In the National Assembly, only the finance committee was to be given authority to propose amendments to money bills. There was no provision for individual members or other committees to table amendment proposals. Moreover, the draft bill required the finance committee to give seven days' notice of any proposed amendment, while the minister of finance would have the right to address the committee before it tabled any amendments. The implications of these procedural hurdles are stark in the context of the National Assembly rules that applied to money bills at that time, which required any such bill to be referred to the finance committee on the day of its introduction (rule 290). Moreover, the rules limited the period for finance committee consideration of money bills to "a maximum of seven consecutive Assembly working days" and required the committee to report to the house before the deadline expired. With these time restrictions, a requirement of seven days' notice for amendments would have eliminated any realistic possibility of change.

In addition, the draft bill sought to prohibit most types of amendments. Without the written consent of the finance minister, the finance committee would not be allowed to table any amendments that increased total spending or spending on a "vote" (an appropriation for a particular department or government entity), or introduced a new expenditure item. Hence, it would have been possible for Parliament to reduce expenditure only on existing items. Amendment authority on the revenue side of the budget was even more restricted. Parliament was not allowed to alter the rate, base or time of imposition of a tax, levy or duty; to introduce any new measures; or to exempt any person from proposed measures. In essence, the draft bill allowed the finance minister to veto any substantive amendments to proposed tax and other revenue measures.

The draft bill faced strong opposition in Parliament and civil society (Krafchik and Wehner 1998). The Congress of South African Trade Unions (Cosatu), despite its electoral alliance with the ANC, strongly condemned the draft bill (Congress of South African Trade Unions 1997), saying that "the restrictive content of the proposed Bill ... is a result of the lack of consultation and public discussion ... In fact, the proposed Bill limits the rights of Parliament to such an extent that it would appear to undermine the spirit, if not the letter, of the constitution's commitment to parliamentary oversight of the budget." A number of ANC MPs were also uneasy about the executive's emphasis on fiscal consolidation, and sympathised with the trade unions' demands for a more interventionist role by the legislature. After all, the ANC's policy platform for the 1994 elections, the Reconstruction and Development Programme, called for an end to "unnecessary secrecy in the formulation of the budget" and the establishment of "a Parliamentary Budget Office with sufficient resources and personnel to ensure efficient democratic oversight of the budget" (African National Congress 1994: 6.5.8).

So united was the criticism of the draft bill that it was withdrawn and never formally tabled. Cosatu decided to boycott parliamentary hearings on the budget until Parliament received meaningful powers of amendment. Together with the South African Council of Churches and the South African NGO Coalition (Sangoco), it formed a People's Budget Campaign in 2000, and over the following years released alternative budget proposals and continued to call for legislation to allow Parliament to amend money bills.

Although there was little progress towards resolving the issue in the following years, other legislative developments somewhat strengthened parliamentary control. In 1999, the Public Finance Management Act (PFMA) replaced the inherited patchwork of ten different Exchequer Acts and gave effect to various sections in the financial chapter of the Constitution. Several provisions of this Act enhanced oversight, including a requirement that budgets include performance information in the form of "measurable objectives" (section 27); numerical limits on the authority of the executive to reallocate funds between programmes during the financial year (section 43); and regular in-year reporting (section 32). This legislation was also noteworthy for the way in which the finance committee took the lead in rewriting the bill, including the insertion of these and many other provisions.[37] Yet the debate on Parliament's amendment powers remained unresolved.

A prolonged stalemate followed, and on occasions, the divisions in the ANC on this issue became publicly visible. In June 2001, Barbara Hogan, then the chairperson of the finance committee, announced that MPs and the finance minister had come to an agreement on parliamentary amendment powers with regard to money bills (Ensor 2001). The tabling of new legislation appeared to be imminent. However, soon afterwards the media reported that Hogan had resigned, citing as her main reason her frustration about the lack of progress towards more substantial parliamentary involvement in the budget process (Ensor 2002). Hogan did continue as chairperson of the finance committee, but the incident highlighted the divisions within the ANC on this matter.

During this time, Parliament also carried out a review of its oversight and accountability functions based on a report by consultants from the University of Cape Town's law faculty (Corder et al. 1999). The joint rules committee tasked a special sub-committee to review the Corder Report. Under the stewardship of Fatima Chohan, the sub-committee developed a set of eight recommendations. With regard to the budget process, it argued that Parliament should develop "an influencing role" and strengthen its "technical capacity". Although it cautioned that "amendments to the budget should be affected only in extreme and extraordinary contingencies", the report went on to recommend the establishment of a "formal process" leading to the enactment of the constitutionally required legislation (Ad Hoc Joint Sub-Committee on Oversight and Accountability 2002: recommendation 8). The joint rules committee subsequently convened a task team on accountability and oversight, and a budget focus group was instructed to develop legislation.

In October 2002, the National Assembly resolved to establish a joint budget committee comprising 15 assembly members and eight members of the National Council of Provinces (Murray and Simeon 1999). The mandate of this new committee was to scrutinise the medium-term expenditure framework and appropriation bill tabled with the annual budget, monthly in-year expenditure and revenue statements, and the pre-budget MTBPS, with the exception of macro-economic and revenue issues. Moreover, the committee was to consider Parliament's role in the development of budgets "in accordance with constitutional requirements". The committee got off to an unambitious start and struggled to develop an active role.[38]

Almost ten years after the failed attempt by the Department of Finance to advance the required legislation, little concrete progress had been made on the issue. Parliament had a new committee, the joint budget committee, but it operated in a vacuum because of the unresolved issue of Parliament's budgetary authority and struggled to establish a meaningful role for itself. It was a case of what Calland (1997) described as "all dressed up with nowhere to go". During this period, some treasury officials started to talk about scrapping the constitutional requirement for legislation on the amendment of money bills as a possible option for resolving the stalemate. As one MP put it, the issue had evolved into a "never-ending battle" with "endless renditions of the bill that just went nowhere" (author's interview).

4. THE NEW FRAMEWORK

Several political changes made the tabling of legislation on parliamentary amendment powers possible in 2008. One was the replacement of the Speaker of the National Assembly, Frene Ginwala, in 2004. Calland (2006: 111) describes her as "executive-minded" and cites an MP from the ruling ANC as saying: "As a manager she was despotic, and resented the growth of the committee system, over which she had insufficient control and which thereby sapped power from the plenary, where she did have full control." Ginwala was also strongly opposed to giving Parliament budgetary amendment powers. According to another MP, she had been "the biggest blockage" in the way of resolving of this issue (author's interview). A second factor was the leadership battle and subsequent realignment of power in the ruling party. During the ANC's Polokwane conference in December 2007, former president Thabo Mbeki lost his bid to remain party leader to his rival and former deputy president, Jacob Zuma. Zuma's victory was immediately felt in Parliament, where it precipitated a changing of the guard. Before the Polokwane conference, ministers dominated the political committee of the ANC, but changes in January 2008 altered its composition and brought in Zuma supporters with substantial parliamentary experience.[39] The balance of power within the party had shifted in favour of strong parliamentary oversight. This paved the way for the National Assembly to formally instruct the finance committee to report a bill by mid-August, based on the work by the task team on oversight and accountability.

A draft Money Bill Amendment Procedure and Related Matters Bill appeared in the Government Gazette in July 2008. Instead of the joint budget committee, it required a committee in each chamber to consider macro-economic and fiscal policy and amendments to money bills (section 4). The finance minister was to submit to Parliament "draft budget allocations for each programme within a vote as approved by Cabinet" at least three months before the budget (section 5). Approval of "the fiscal framework" and the annual Division of Revenue Bill regulating transfers and grants to the provinces and local governments was required before consideration of any amendments to the budget (section 6). The draft bill did not contain specific limits on amendments, but required members to motivate these with reference to a list of 11 items, starting with "the relevant fiscal framework adopted by Parliament" (section 7). Ministers were to be given 30 days to comment before committees could consider adopting amendments. The budget committees would be required to report within four months after the introduction of the relevant money bill. If Parliament failed to adopt any amendments within this period, it would have to adopt the bill as tabled. Finally, the draft bill provided for the establishment of a parliamentary budget office as part of the parliamentary administration (section 8). These proposals envisaged a substantial restructuring of the budgetary role of Parliament, but they were also imprecise in some important aspects, notably the definition of "the fiscal framework" and the distinction between the revenue and expenditure side of the budget.

Following public hearings, the finance committee revised the draft and formally tabled the Money Bills Amendment Procedure and Related Matters Bill, which was passed into law (Act No. 9 of 2009). The new legislation clarifies several aspects. Notably, it defines the fiscal framework as comprising aggregate spending and revenues (budgetary and extra-budgetary), as well as borrowing, interest and debt servicing charges and the contingency reserve (section 1). It also clearly distinguishes the revenue and expenditure sides of the budget, and assigns responsibility for them to different sets of committees. The scrutiny of macro-economic and fiscal policy, as well as revenue measures, fell to the existing finance committees, whereas a new set of appropriations committees, one in each house, would scrutinise spending and the intergovernmental division of revenue (section 4).

In addition, the Act establishes a clear sequence of decisions. It tasks portfolio committees with producing "budgetary review and recommendation reports" for each department (section 5) before the adoption of reports on the MTBPS prepared by the finance and appropriation committees after its tabling in the spring (section 6). Reports on the MTBPS could include recommendations for amendments to the fiscal framework or the division of revenue should they remain "materially unchanged" when submitted with the budget towards the beginning of autumn. The approval of the annual budget was to start with the adoption of the fiscal framework and revenue proposals (section 8), followed by the Division of Revenue Bill (section 9) and, finally, the relevant appropriation bill (section 10). The minister of finance was given the right to respond to proposed amendments of these within at least two, three and ten days respectively. In the case of amendments to appropriations, any affected cabinet member also received the right to respond. The Act required any amendments to appropriations, revenue measures and the division of revenue to be consistent with the adopted fiscal framework and several guiding principles, which are reproduced in Appendix 2 of this book. In short, the Act established a top-down process for budgetary decisions.

The Act also included new instruments for parliamentary control (section 10), which had not been in the draft gazetted in 2008. Over the years of work on this issue, some MPs had obtained examples of legislative budget processes in other countries, including Germany. The German Parliament has powers to insert a "qualified freeze", which requires the federal ministry of finance to obtain parliamentary consent before the budgeted amount for a particular item, or a certain percentage of it, can be spent. This requires the provision of additional information to the budget committee, until MPs are satisfied and release the funds (Eickenboom 1989: 1208). Drawing on this experience, the South African legislation allowed other committees to recommend to an appropriations committee that a sub-division of a main division within a vote be appropriated "conditionally", "to ensure that the money requested for the main division will be spent effectively, efficiently and economically". Incidentally, the only amendment the National Assembly made to the bill was to remove a limitation on the sum of money that could be appropriated conditionally.[40] In addition, the Act allowed other committees to advise the appropriations committees that money be appropriated "specifically and exclusively" for a particular main division within a vote, thereby suspending the virement rules in the PFMA (section 43) for specific items. These provisions enable a high degree of control over budget execution.

Finally, the Act also significantly overhauls the provisions on the establishment of the parliamentary budget office (section 15). Notably, it stipulates as its main objective the provision of "independent, objective and professional advice and analysis to Parliament on matters related to the budget and other money Bills". While the draft bill as gazetted envisaged that the office would be established by the secretary to Parliament as part of the parliamentary administration, the Act gives the finance and appropriations committees the duty of recommending to their respective houses the appointment of "a person with the requisite experience, qualifications and leadership skills" as director. It defines the position at the same level as the top rank of the public service. The director can only be removed from office in case of "misconduct, incapacity or incompetence", as attested by the appointing committees, and with the adoption of a resolution to that effect by both houses. The independence of the office is underscored by a requirement that the director report to Parliament "any inappropriate political or executive interference" in the fulfilment of its mandate, and substantial financial and operational independence. In short, the Act envisages an independent and well-resourced analytic unit to support the new process.

The second attempt to establish a procedure for the amendment of money bills was considerably more successful than the first in 1997. The Act outlines a firm top-down budget procedure, clearly defines the tasks of the different committees, and provides a framework for the establishment of an independent analytic unit. Many elements in the Act go beyond the draft gazetted earlier in asserting Parliament's authority, and overall it provides a powerful set of tools for legislative engagement with the budget.

5. Conclusions

For more than a decade after the adoption of a democratic constitution, the budgetary role of South Africa's legislatures remained undefined, as the ruling party was unable to reconcile conflicting visions of parliamentary involvement. The 1997 draft bill on the amendment process for money bills would have severely curtailed Parliament's authority, to an extent that many parliamentarians and civil society organisations deemed unacceptable. In contrast, the 2009 Money Bills Amendment Procedure and Related Matters Act pursues a more modern approach. On the one hand, the choice of unfettered amendment authority; additional tools to control the execution of the budget; the establishment of well-defined financial committees; and the creation of the parliamentary budget office marked a shift away from weak and passive scrutiny of the budget. At the same time, the legislation introduced procedural safeguards, notably a committee structure similar to the "hierarchical" model in Figure 2, as well as a requirement that Parliament fix key fiscal aggregates before making decisions that are consistent with it.

Without a doubt, the legislation is a major milestone and represents a leap forward in the evolution of South Africa's democratic institutions. It frees the parliamentary process from some of the most restrictive aspects of its Westminster heritage, and has the potential to facilitate active legislative participation in budgetary decisions. Moreover, the new framework was carefully crafted in an attempt to reconcile strong legislative control of the budget process with prudent fiscal management. Of course, the effectiveness of the procedural safeguards may not be revealed immediately. It is the confluence of political and institutional fragmentation that constitutes the greatest threat to prudent fiscal policy (Wehner 2008). When a governing party commands a secure majority in the legislature, the design of budgetary procedures is arguably less important, as party discipline is enough to contain amendment activity. Only a more fragmented political context would reveal the true efficacy of the new process.

References

Abedian, I., T. Ajam and L. Walker, *Promises, Plans and Priorities: South Africa's Emerging Fiscal Structures*, Cape Town, Idasa, 1997.

Ad Hoc Joint Sub-Committee on Oversight and Accountability. *Final Report*. Cape Town, Parliament of South Africa, 2002.

African National Congress. *The Reconstruction and Development Programme: A Policy Framework*, Johannesburg, Umanyano Publications, 1994.

Alesina, A., R. Hausmann, R. Hommes and E. Stein, "Budget Institutions and Fiscal

Performance in Latin America", *Journal of Development Economics* 59(2) 1999: 253-273.

Breton, A., *Competitive Governments: An Economic Theory of Politics and Public Finance*. Cambridge, Cambridge University Press, 1996.

Calland, R., "All Dressed up with Nowhere to Go? The Rapid Transformation of the South African Parliamentary Committee System (in Comparative Theoretical Perspective)", Bellville, School of Government, University of the Western Cape, 1997.

Calland, R., *The First Five Years: A Review of South Africa's Democratic Parliament*, Cape Town, Idasa, 1999.

Calland, R., *Anatomy of South Africa: Who holds the Power?* Cape Town, Zebra Press, 2006.

Congress of South African Trade Unions, *Cosatu Submission on the Money Bills Amendment Procedure Bill*, presented to the portfolio committee on finance, 22 October 1997. Cape Town, Congress of South African Trade Unions.

Coombes, D. L., (ed.) *The Power of the Purse: The Role of European Parliaments in Budgetary Decisions*, London, George Allen and Unwin, 1976.

Corder, H., S. Jagwanth and F. Soltau, *Report on Parliamentary Oversight and Accountability*, Cape Town, Faculty of Law, University of Cape Town, 1999.

Crain, M. W. and T. J. Muris, "Legislative Organization of Fiscal Policy", *Journal of Law and Economics* 38(2) 1995: 311-333.

Department of Finance, *Medium Term Budget Policy Statement*, Pretoria, Government Printer, 1997.

Department of Finance, *Growth, Employment and Redistribution: A Macroeconomic Strategy*, Pretoria, Government Printer, 1996.

Ehrhart, K.-M., R. Gardner, J. von Hagen and C. Keser, "Budget Processes: Theory and Experimental Evidence", *Games and Economic Behavior* 59(2) 2007: 279-295.

Eickenboom, P., *Haushaltsausschuß und Haushaltsverfahren. Parlamentsrecht und Parlamentspraxis in der Bundesrepublik Deutschland: Ein Handbuch*. H.-P. Schneider and W. Zeh. Berlin, De Gruyter 1989: 1183-1220.

Einzig, P., *The Control of the Purse: Progress and Decline of Parliament's Financial Control*, London, Secker and Warburg, 1959.

Ensor, L., "Manuel and MPs Agree on Powers to Affect Budget", *Business Day*, 27 June 2001, Johannesburg: 2.

Ensor, L., "Hogan Resigns from Finance Committee", *Business Day*, 29 May 2002, Johannesburg: 1.

Fabrizio, S. and A. Mody, "Can Budget Institutions Counteract Political Indiscipline?", *Economic Policy* 21(48) 2006: 690-739.

Ferejohn, J. and K. Krehbiel, "The Budget Process and the Size of the Budget", *American Journal of Political Science* 31(2) 1987: 296-320.

Feinstein, A. *After the Party: A Personal and Political Journey Inside the ANC*, Johannesburg, Jonathan Ball, 2007.

Filc, G. and C. Scartascini, "Budget Institutions and Fiscal Outcomes: Ten Years of Inquiry on Fiscal Matters at the Research Department", Paper presented at the IADB Research Department Ten-Year Anniversary Conference, 17 September 2004. Washington, D. C., Inter-American Development Bank.

Hallerberg, M. and J. Von Hagen, "Sequencing and the Size of the Budget: A Reconsideration", Centre for Economic Policy Research Discussion Paper 1589, 1997.

Hallerberg, M. and P. Marier, "Executive Authority, the Personal Vote, and Budget Discipline in Latin American and Caribbean Countries", *American Journal of Political Science* 48(3) 2004: 571-587.

Hallerberg, M., R. Strauch and J. Von Hagen, "The Design of Fiscal Rules and Forms of Governance in European Union Countries", *European Journal of Political Economy* 23(2) 2007: 338-359.

International Monetary Fund, *South Africa: Staff Report for the 2003 Article IV Consultation*, Washington, D. C., International Monetary Fund, 2003.

Kotzé, H., *The New Parliament: Transforming the Westminster Heritage. South Africa: Designing New Political Institutions*, M. Faure and J.-E. Lane (eds.), London, Sage (1996): 252-268.

Krafchik, W. and J. Wehner, "The Role of Parliament in the Budgetary Process", *South African Journal of Economics* 66(4) 1998: 512-541.

Lienert, I., "Who Controls the Budget: The Legislature or the Executive?" IMF Working Paper WP/05/115, 2005.

Meyers, R. T., "Will the U.S. Congress's 'Power of the Purse' Become Unexceptional?" Paper presented at the Annual Meeting of the American Political Science Association, San Francisco, 2001.

Michie, J. and V. Padayachee, "Three Years after Apartheid: Growth, Employment and Redistribution?", *Cambridge Journal of Economics* 22 1998: 623-635.

Murray, C. and L. Nijzink, "Building Representative Democracy: South Africa's Legislatures and the Constitution", Cape Town, European Union Parliamentary Support Programme, 2002.

Murray, C. M. and R. Simeon, "From Paper to Practice: The National Council of Provinces after its First Year", *SA Public Law* 14(1) 1999: 96-141.

Newham, G., "Legislature Battles the Budget", *Parliamentary Whip*, 11 August 1997, Cape Town, Idasa: 2-3.

Oppenheimer, B. I., "How Legislatures Shape Policy and Budgets", *Legislative Studies Quarterly* 8(4) 1983: 551-597.

Organisation for Economic Co-operation and Development and World Bank, "Results of the Survey on Budget Practices and Procedures", available at www.oecd.org/gov/budget/database, 2003.

Perotti, R. and Y. Kontopoulos "Fragmented Fiscal Policy", *Journal of Public Economics* 86(2) 2002: 191-222.

Schick, A., "Can National Legislatures Regain an Effective Voice in Budget Policy?" *OECD Journal on Budgeting* 1(3) 2002: 15-42.

Stourm, R., *The Budget*, New York and London, D. Appleton for the Institute for

Government Research, 1917.

Streak, J. "The Gear Legacy: Did Gear Fail or Move South Africa Forward in Development?" *Development Southern Africa* 21(2) 2004: 271-288.

Velasco, A, "Debts and Deficits with Fragmented Fiscal Policymaking", *Journal of Public Economics* 76(1) 2000: 105-125.

Von Hagen, J., *Budgeting Procedures and Fiscal Performance in the European Communities*, Brussels, Directorate-General for Economic and Financial Affairs, Commission of the European Communities, 1992.

Von Hagen, J. and I. J. Harden, "Budget Processes and Commitment to Fiscal Discipline", *European Economic Review* 39(3) 1995: 771-779.

Walker, L. and B. Mengistu, *Spend and Deliver: A Guide to the Medium-Term Expenditure Framework*, Cape Town, Idasa, 1999.

Weeks, J., "Stuck in Low GEAR? Macroeconomic Policy in South Africa, 1996-1998", *Cambridge Journal of Economics* 23(6) 1999: 795-811.

Wehner, J., "Assessing the Power of the Purse: An Index of Legislative Budget Institutions", *Political Studies* 54(4) 2006: 767-785.

Wehner, J., "Budget Reform and Legislative Control in Sweden", *Journal of European Public Policy* 14(2) 2007: 313-332.

Wehner, J., "Institutional Constraints on Profligate Politicians: The Conditional Effect of Partisan Fragmentation on Budget Deficits", *Comparative Political Studies* (forthcoming), 2008. Working paper version available at http://papers.ssrn.com/sol3/papers.cfm?abstract_id=1281082

Weingast, B. R., K. A. Shepsle and C. Johnsen, "The Political Economy of Benefits and Costs: A Neoclassical Approach to Distributive Politics", *Journal of Political Economy* 89(4) 1981: 642-664.

Yläoutinen, S., *Fiscal Frameworks in the Central and Eastern European Countries*, Helsinki, Ministry of Finance, 2004.

Chapter 3

Budget oversight and poverty alleviation: opportunities and challenges

Tania Ajam

1. INTRODUCTION

Poverty and inequality are among the major challenges facing South African society, and the major thrust of policy in all spheres of government. In his 2002 state of the nation address, former president Thabo Mbeki reaffirmed government's commitment to poverty alleviation through concrete, time-specific programmes, and called on all organs of state to reflect on their role in promoting anti-poverty objectives. "Of decisive importance," Mbeki remarked, was the question of whether the legislature, executive and judiciary, as well as civil society, are effectively "helping to lift from the shoulders of our people the intolerable burden of poverty and underdevelopment" (Mbeki, 2002). The goals of combating poverty and inequality have underpinned successive government programmes of action and their pursuit is likely to be intensified under President Jacob Zuma's administration.

The Constitution confers justiciable socio-economic rights on all citizens, which must be progressively realised within available resource constraints. This has and will continue to play a major role in poverty alleviation. South Africa is also a signatory to a number of international commitments to eliminate poverty and inequality, including the Millennium Development Goals and conventions on the rights of women and children.

Internationally, there is a growing consensus that good governance can promote pro-poor distributive outcomes and reduce corruption (United Nations Development Programme, 1998). Budgets are particularly powerful instruments in socio-economic transformation, redirecting public resources to benefit the poor and other vulnerable groups, particularly in the provision of public services. Non-delivery, inefficiency, waste and corruption often have a disproportionately negative effect on these groups. Furthermore, there is a growing recognition of the role of legislatures and Parliament as key facilitators of effective, politically legitimate and sustainable poverty reduction strategies (Hlubi and Mandaville, 2004: ODI, 2007).

The budget process is unique in that it strives to integrate, in an over-arching framework, the governance choices of the whole of government and the individual policy choices of each sector in a concrete, regular and reliable way. Far from being merely a technical accounting process, it is inherently and intensely political. Without such a process, there can be no meaningful political debate on the appropriateness of choices proposed by government, possible alternatives, the responsibilities of decision-makers, or the coherence and integration of diverse policies supporting over-arching goals such as poverty alleviation.

The core functions of the legislature – legislation, representation and oversight – can be a vehicle for encouraging policy formulation, legislation and implementation aimed at poverty alleviation. Whether legislatures have the space, authority, capacity, incentive and inclination to do this depends on a range of factors. This chapter draws on international experience, and examines some of the major factors which have impinged on the effective fiscal oversight of legislatures and their ability to help generate policy aimed at supporting the poor and other vulnerable groups in society.

2. The legislature and fiscal oversight in South Africa

The optimal role of legislatures in engaging with fiscal policy and the budget is the subject of fierce debate internationally, but most countries acknowledge that legislatures do have a fiscal oversight role in promoting the wise stewardship of public resources and efficient service delivery. However, the exact parameters of that role diverge across countries, as do the systems, procedures, governance structures and political culture in which that role is played.

In emerging democracies, in conditions where even the rule of law may be fragile, a key challenge is building an effective institutional identity for legislatures. In established democracies, legislatures grapple with redefining their traditional roles in the wake of far-reaching budget and broader public sector reform initiatives, which have profoundly changed the fiscal landscape in which they must operate. At the same time, organised civil society groups and informed citizens are exerting greater pressure on legislatures to be more exacting in discharging their oversight responsibilities.

2.1 Historical background

In apartheid South Africa, budgeting and the budget process were characterised by secrecy and lack of transparency, with negligible participation by Parliament or civil society. The criteria and rationale for the allocation of public funds were never explicitly articulated. During this period, the legislature was completely overshadowed by the executive. Parliament had no power to change the budget proposed by cabinet and its role was limited to that of a rubber stamp.

The budgeting system itself was *ad hoc* and incremental, with minimal forward planning or performance orientation. Budget documents were highly inaccessible and user-unfriendly, making it possible to exercise a degree of financial control over public funds spent but not over *how* these funds were spent – that is, whether they were spent effectively. The inherently secretive and unaccountable nature of the budget system was further entrenched by the obscuring of details of expenditure on certain clandestine items, such as the activities of the military, police and "sanctions-busting."

Under apartheid, even the involvement of elected officials in the executive in budgeting was minimal. As described by Fubbs (2001), budgets were historically "driven by technicians and the administration, with little if any political intervention and an implicit policy of producing documentation that made it impossible for the public to appreciate the purpose of expenditure and the achievements of objectives".

After the transition to democracy in 1994, innovations including the medium-term expenditure framework (MTEF) and the minister's committee on the budget were introduced,[41] among other things, to enhance political oversight of resource allocation. National and provincial MTEFs outline planned spending activities and revenue targets over a three-year horizon. This potentially gives Parliament, provincial legislatures and civil society a greater opportunity to engage with and influence the prioritisation of future spending. This is discussed in greater detail below.

2.2 THE SOUTH AFRICAN CONSTITUTION

Any attempt to explore the role of the legislature in the budget process in contemporary South Africa must take the Constitution as its point of departure.

2.2.1 LEGISLATURES AND SOCIO-ECONOMIC RIGHTS

The South African Constitution is unique in that the Bill of Rights, in Chapter 2, commits the state to the progressive realisation of a range of socio-economic rights, including housing, healthcare, education and social security, within available resources. The role of the state in fulfilling these rights is confirmed in section 7, and section 8 makes this obligation explicitly binding on the legislature, executive, judiciary and other organs of state. The legislature, as a crucial governance institution, is thus obliged to promote and fulfil these rights while carrying out the core functions of legislation, representation and oversight.

These rights are justiciable and can be legally enforced, and have already been tested in several high-profile Constitutional Court cases with public resource implications.[42] However, Murray and Nijzink also observe that the "protection of the Constitution and human rights" are "not the preserve of the courts". The authors suggest, rather, that legislatures are "institutions that oversee the development and implementation of policy. They must be proactive in developing a democratic rights culture and must be central agents in the realisation of rights and the transformation of the country" (Murray and Nijzink, 2002:3).

2.2.2 FISCAL GOVERNANCE

Section 185 of the Constitution also envisages a public service that is development-orientated, responsive, accountable and transparent, and which actively engages the public in policy-making processes. This applies to all three spheres of government.

Chapter 13 of the Constitution addresses issues of finance and the "fiscal constitution", referring to the rules and principles by which budgetary decisions are made, implemented and accounted for. Chapter 13 further outlines the revenue-raising authority of the spheres of government, revenue-sharing and intergovernmental grants and borrowing powers. Schedules 4 and 5 deal with the concurrent and exclusive functions of sub-national governments, which determine their expenditure responsibilities.

Section 216 entrenches the principles of good fiscal governance, such as transparency and accountability in budget processes and effective financial management of budget implementation.[43] Section 188 also establishes the office of an independent Auditor-General, who must submit reports to the relevant national or provincial legislatures.

2.2.3   FISCAL OVERSIGHT

A number of different sections of the Constitution are also relevant to the task of fiscal oversight.

Section 55 outlines the powers of the National Assembly, including that of passing legislation. National budgets are classified as "money bills", and while the National Assembly may pass such bills, it is explicitly prohibited from initiating or preparing them by section 55 (1)(b). Section 114 (1) imposes the same restriction on provincial legislatures.

Section 77 defines money bills as those that appropriate money; impose taxes, levies, duties or surcharges, or abolish, reduce or grant exemptions to these; and authorise direct charges against the National Revenue Fund. Section 77 (3) also establishes procedures for the consideration of money bills, and importantly, specifies that an "Act of Parliament must provide for a procedure to amend money bills before Parliament". Again, an analogous definition for a provincial money bill is included in section 120.

However, no province has passed legislation allowing for budgetary amendments of this kind, nor, until 2009, was comparable legislation passed at national level. Murray and Nijzink suggest that this reflects the "delicate balance of power between the legislature and the executive that the legislation must capture and the big stakes that both the legislature and the executive must attach to the issue. Money bills – and particularly the bundle of bills that make up the annual budget – encapsulate government's policy agenda in a more concrete way than any other pieces of legislation" (Murray and Nijzink, 2002: 97).

Thus, while the Constitution clearly intends a role for the legislature in amending budgets, its scope will be reflected in enabling legislation. The design of legislation that fleshes out the Constitution will be one of the few factors shaping the legislature's role in the budget process. Other factors, discussed later, will certainly be influential in shaping its institutional development, but will be largely exogenous to the legislature.

There is also an important role for the National Council of Provinces (NCOP) in the intergovernmental budget process. Section 214 of the Constitution requires an Act of Parliament to provide for the equitable division of national revenue between the three spheres of government; the determination of each province's equitable share of national revenue; and any other allocations to the provinces, local government or municipalities.

Oversight of budget execution is located in Parliament's broader responsibility to monitor implementation of legislation and policy, also captured in sections 55 and 114. Corresponding with the duty imposed on provincial legislatures to hold the executive to account, the Constitution also emphasises the accountability of individual ministers and executive councils as a whole to the national Parliament.

Section 92 further outlines the accountability and responsibility of the deputy president, ministers and cabinet members, and specifies that the latter are accountable "collectively and individually to Parliament for the exercise of their powers and the performance of their functions". Section 133 outlines the comparable roles and responsibilities at provincial level.

Section 56 also allows the National Assembly and portfolio committees to call people to give evidence under oath or to produce documents, and to receive petitions, representations and submissions from interested parties or institutions. Similar provisions apply to provincial legislatures and committees in section 115.

In this way, the Constitution clarifies some dimensions of fiscal accountability, such as access to information and the requirement that ministers and executive councils explain their policies. However, some areas of fiscal oversight remain unclear, for instance in respect of amendatory accountability. This refers to the "duty inherent in the concept of accountability, to rectify or make good any shortcoming or mistake uncovered" (Corder et al., 1999).

Ministerial responsibility has several dimensions, to which escalating sanctions may be applied. These include informatory responsibility, or the obligation to keep Parliament informed of the operation of departments; explanatory responsibility, to explain and defend government policy to Parliament and the public; amendatory responsibility, requiring that mistakes made in good faith are admitted to Parliament and remedial measures proposed; and resignatory responsibility, requiring resignation for egregious ineptitude or corruption, disagreement with the cabinet or policy, bringing the ruling party or the cabinet into disrepute, and lying to Parliament (Sennay and Besdziek, 1999).

No constitutional provisions define the degree of responsibility of ministers and civil servants. The role of civil servants has been clarified in legislation, including the Public Finance Management Act of 1999 (PFMA) and management tools including performance contracts, but the extent of ministerial accountability remains largely unexplored. For example, section 63 of the PFMA requires ministers to stay within their budgets, but no sanctions are attached, as they are to accounting officers, as this is presumed to be dealt with by an undefined political process.

2.3 LEGISLATIVE FRAMEWORKS FOR PUBLIC FINANCIAL AND PERFORMANCE MANAGEMENT

To give operational substance to the constitutional provisions discussed above, the PFMA initiated a move from an input-oriented expenditure control system to a more performance-orientated system that supports oversight of service delivery and spending. The PFMA set out to modernise public sector budgeting and financial management through regular financial reporting, sound internal expenditure controls, independent audit and supervision of control systems, improved accounting standards and training of financial managers, and greater emphasis on outputs and performance monitoring.

In 2003, the Municipal Finance Management Act (MFMA) extended budget reform to local government. It complemented existing legislation such as the Municipal Systems Act of 2000, which dealt with municipal planning (integrated development plans) and performance management systems.

Since 1994, the quality, timeliness and comprehensiveness of fiscal data have improved markedly. Data are regularly published in the annual national, provincial and local budget reviews, and are freely available on the National Treasury website. The introduction of the medium-term budget policy statement (MTBPS) from 1997 has improved debt and cash management strategies. It states government's aggregate revenue and expenditure intentions over the next three years and includes indicative figures on the division of revenue among provincial governments.

Multi-year budgeting, also used in the United Kingdom, had its genesis in the PFMA and was put into effect through the MTEF in 1998/99. It provides for three-year rolling budgets for the national and provincial governments in March, as well as underlying macro-economic projections. Since 1999, the budget has been tabled before the start of the financial year. A new budget and reporting format was introduced in 2004, aligned with the International Public Accounting Standards issued by the International Federation of Accountants, and based on a new standard chart of accounts (National Treasury, 2004: vii).

Other significant milestones in the evolution of intergovernmental fiscal relations include the creation of the Budget Council in 1996, which presides over the revenue-sharing process, and the establishment of formula-based revenue sharing recommended by the Financial and Fiscal Commission. The Intergovernmental Fiscal Relations Act of 1997 also introduced predictability and transparency in the intergovernmental budget process.

The annual Division of Revenue Bill formalises revenue-sharing across the three spheres of government, and provides three-year projections of both unconditional equitable share grants and conditional grants to provinces and municipalities. The Intergovernmental Relations Framework Act of 2005 establishes the legislative framework for intergovernmental relations and the roles and functions of national, provincial and municipal intergovernmental forums, and stipulates the conduct relating to the implementation protocols and procedures for resolving intergovernmental disputes.

This legislative framework, along with the PFMA, gives Parliament and provincial legislatures timely and credible oversight tools. Before the PFMA took effect, credible in-year financial reporting was virtually non-existent, and there was no early warning system to detect in-year overspending or underspending. This clearly undermined effective oversight of budget execution. Furthermore, there was often a lag of up to two years before audited financial statements were available to the public accounts committees of Parliament and provincial legislatures. The PFMA requires that financial statements are produced no later than three months after the end of the financial year, and that they are audited no more than seven months after year-end.

The implementation of the PFMA initially focused on improving financial reporting and management systems and procedures, but this has gradually been expanded to include analysis in terms of efficiency and effectiveness, requiring non-financial information on service delivery. As well as tabling annual budgets in Parliament and the provincial legislatures, ministers and members of executive councils must table strategic plans and/or annual performance plans for scrutiny and approval. Linking output measures, framed in measurable objectives, to resource allocation is crucial in creating an orientation towards value for money. These plans and budgets lay the foundation for in-year monthly and quarterly financial reporting, as well as year-end annual reports and audited financial statements. Each of these instruments is crucial for effective oversight of budgetary execution.

Since 2003, the National Treasury has also engaged extensively with provincial government departments in instituting standardised five-year strategic plans, annual performance plans and quarterly performance reports that monitor service delivery progress and spending against plans. In May 2007, Treasury published its *Framework for Managing Programme Performance Information* which, among other things, clarified standards and definitions for performance information in support of the auditing of non-financial information.

This framework, with Statistics South Africa's South African Statistics Quality Assurance Framework, supports the Presidency's Government-Wide Monitory and Evaluation Policy Framework, released in 2007. The latter addresses challenges to government effectiveness, envisaging monitoring and evaluation processes that assist the public sector in evaluating performance and achieving service delivery outcomes. Monitoring and evaluation aims to draw causal connections between the choice of policy priorities, resourcing, programmes designed to implement them, services actually delivered, and their impact on communities. Evaluations are also potentially important instruments of legislative oversight.

Performance information and monitoring and evaluation frameworks will ultimately enable the Auditor-General to audit non-financial information, assuring Parliament that the service delivery achievements reported by line departments can be verified. In the past, the Auditor-General focused on financial and compliance audits, and expressed an opinion on whether financial statements prepared by departments fairly reflect their financial position and activities. Internationally, public sector reforms have increasingly emphasised both financial and non-financial reporting to Parliaments and legislatures. National Treasury regulations now require that annual reports of national and provincial government departments include audited financial statements and statements of programme performance.

Section 20 (1)(c) of the Public Audit Act of 2004 requires the Auditor-General to express an opinion or conclusion on "reported information of the auditee against pre-determined objectives", fulfilling a verification function and assuring Parliament of the accuracy of non-financial information. Rather than on outcome and impact data, the Auditor-General's focus will, therefore, be on non-financial information included in annual reports for accountability purposes and output-related non-financial data, as these constitute the locus of accountability for accounting officers. A major focus will also be on departmental implementation of systems for managing performance information, and the implementation of robust internal controls to ensure their integrity.

Although it is easier to monitor and evaluate service delivery output data, it is important that Parliament and the legislatures continue focusing on the link between these outputs and the achievement of policy outcomes. This relationship is complex and influenced by many exogenous factors. But it is crucial that the assumptions, risks and causal relationships underlying policy and programme logic and proposed delivery mechanisms are made explicit at the stage of conceptualisation. Furthermore, at the execution stage, ongoing oversight can ensure that these risks are managed; that implementation is focused and goal-directed; and that the intended beneficiaries are reached. Legislative oversight of implementation can ensure that pro-poor and gender-sensitive policies are applied as intended, and that there is adequate consultation with low-income or vulnerable beneficiary groups in formulating and implementing policy, programmes or projects.

In conclusion, the constitutional perspective on oversight covers the entire scope of legislative activity, to ensure that laws are implemented in a way that realises their intention. In fiscal oversight in particular, the legislature's role is not confined to the appropriation process, but includes ensuring congruency between the intentions and outcomes of budgets. Parliament and provincial legislatures were clearly envisaged as having both a prior and follow-up oversight role. Parliament's role in the budget formulation process improves engagement with policy debates in respect of planned aggregate fiscal discipline, namely appropriate levels of taxation, total expenditure and levels of deficit and debt. It also enables Parliament and the legislatures to ensure that both cross-sector macro-prioritisation and micro-prioritisation support poverty eradication objectives. There are always, however, competing demands on limited fiscal resources. Strong political involvement is needed to guide the technical allocation of public funds. The budgeting system should, therefore, accommodate an adequate interplay of technical and political role-players. The larger the disparity between available fiscal resources and the aggregate demand on the fiscus, the greater the need for political guidance in allocative decisions.

In a democracy, achieving allocative efficiency is the platform for enforcing political accountability. Interventions by Parliament to align public spending priorities with the needs and preferences of the poor makes for greater allocative efficiency.[44] Poor people in South Africa and elsewhere often have limited ability and resources to voice their needs and preferences. Through outreach programmes such as "Taking Parliament to the People", Parliament and the legislatures, as representative bodies, can actively solicit the input of poor people and civil society organisations. This input should be channelled to the executive at the most appropriate points in the budget cycle.

To exercise oversight in support of poverty reduction, legislatures must ensure that initiatives to expand access to resources, opportunities and income-earning potential for the poor are budgeted and planned for and carried out, so that there is an impact on the intended beneficiaries. Amending the budget should be a last resort. The preferred alternative is for Parliament to act on the MTEF projections in outer years, as this encourages reprioritisation while minimising disruption at the tail-end of the budget process. In the amendments it proposes, Parliament should balance the need for accelerated quality delivery with the capacity of government institutions and the requirements of prudent stewardship of public resources and fiscal responsibility.

In exercising *ex post facto* oversight of service delivery and budgetary execution, Parliament can ensure that aggregate fiscal discipline is maintained in line with planned expenditure, revenue and deficit totals. Crucially, this means that there should be no deviation from planned budget totals or in respect of individual expenditure categories. For example, overspending on educational personnel could crowd out the provision of learner support materials to poor schools. Underspending of conditional grants is equally problematic, as it often means that government's plans to improve services, or extend these to poor areas, are undermined.

Ongoing follow-up oversight also enables Parliament and the legislatures to create a disincentive for unproductive, fruitless and wasteful expenditure by public institutions. Portfolio committees can actively examine and monitor mechanisms of service delivery to ensure that they are effective, efficient and reach poor beneficiaries. Parliament, specifically through public accounts committees, can also play an important role in combating outright corruption and strengthening integrity systems in the private sector. However, to be effective, Parliament and legislatures must ensure that their own operations, and the conduct of individual parliamentarians, builds their credibility as champions of clean governance among voters.

3. OVERSIGHT MECHANISMS SUPPORTING POVERTY REDUCTION

As discussed above, the Constitution envisages a role for the legislature both in influencing the budget and exercising oversight to ensure the effectiveness, efficiency and economy of service delivery, and that public spending is translated into positive impacts on poor communities. This requires the political will to forge an institutional identity that transcends party politics. The executive must also acknowledge the importance of effective legislative oversight, especially in the context of a strong majority party and limited electoral contestation in the short term. A suitable legislative framework must be put in place, accompanied by the building of capacity to fulfil this function and the internal restructuring of the legislature.

Most importantly, a political culture must be developed which does not regard legislative oversight as a nuisance or an attempt to undermine the executive's ability to govern. Oversight should be seen as a constructive, critical process that enhances the alignment of the budget with human rights priorities and fosters targeted service delivery in favour of poor communities. Similarly, legislators should accept that constructive oversight is not a heresy against their party, but a constitutional duty and moral obligation to the poor electorate they represent.

Currently, national government and some provinces have strong treasuries and political leadership, which could exercise effective oversight of delivery. But as this may not hold true in future, it would be wise to diversify forms of oversight and craft a more robust institutional framework. Even treasuries are limited in what they can do about the shortcomings of line departments, as they are increasingly supposed to be "referees" that enforce the "rules" of the "budget game", rather than active players. Treasuries may compile departmental submissions for a budget document, but are often unable to comment publicly on what they contain.

Finally, such a framework should consider broader governance reforms required to mitigate disincentives for legislators who are responsible for fiscal oversight.

3.1 FORMAL OVERSIGHT POWERS OVER BUDGET IMPLEMENTATION

The 1999 Report on Parliamentary Oversight and Accountability recommended that an Accountability Standards Act be passed to complement the PFMA by setting clear parameters in which committee members should operate (Corder et al., 1999). It would clarify issues of amendatory accountability, standards of administrative accountability, prescribed reporting standards and procedures on receipt of reports, as well as strengthen individual members and committees in performing these roles.

An important precondition for effective oversight is a common understanding of political, as opposed to managerial, accountability. A delicate balance has to be struck between allowing public managers with increased decision-making power in increasingly complex administrative environments to hide behind ministers or to be paralysed by risk aversion, and preventing ministers from using director-generals as scapegoats.

The PFMA affords protection in principle, but this may not translate into protection in practice.[45] Interestingly, PFMA guidelines for accounting officers emphasise that ministers and Members of Executive Council (MECs) are responsible for outcomes, and accounting officers for outputs. However, the legislation itself does not mention outputs or outcomes at all: they appear only in the explanatory memorandum. The nature of ministerial accountability, therefore, remains unclear. The PFMA's regulations provide some additional clarity on the lines of political and managerial accountability, but the Act says far less than the MFMA on the subject of undue political interference. This could be rectified by amending the PFMA.

In recent years, Parliament has been more rigorous in scrutinising public spending and service delivery, as reflected in the media and committee reports, and this encouraging trend should be strengthened (Hartley, 2007; I-Net Bridget, 2008). For instance, Parliament has increasingly refused to allow junior officials to account for service delivery and value-for-money concerns. On occasions, strategic and operational plans, budgets, monthly financial reports and quarterly reports have been used to engage effectively with departments and other public sector institutions, although the quality of oversight varies from committee to committee.

The challenge facing Parliament is how to institutionalise a culture of effective, critical and constructive oversight. A number of decisions must be made at strategic level. For instance, what is the NCOP's oversight role, relative to that of the National Assembly? What specific contribution can the NCOP make in adding value to pro-poor monitoring? How does NCOP oversight differ from that of provincial legislatures? For example, the National Assembly and provincial legislatures could focus on the institutional accountability of departments and public sector institutions, while the NCOP could take a sector-based approach to accountability, with oversight cutting across all spheres of government and public entities. This would ensure the coordination of pro-poor policy, the alignment of fragmented budgets, the compatibility of approaches to service delivery approaches, and sector-wide monitoring and evaluation processes.

For example, if public transport and the built environment are regarded as a sector, the plans and budgets of all role-players could be scrutinised. Once strategic decisions have been made on the macro-oversight model for all legislative institutions, the roles and responsibilities of various role-players could be reviewed to ensure alignment. This could include, for example, the division of labour between the National Assembly's finance committee, the NCOP's select committee on finance, the joint budget committees, the standing committee on public accounts and sector committees.

3.2 POLITICAL CULTURE AND INCENTIVES

The informal rules and conventions surrounding institutions are probably more powerful than formal rules. An institution with a strong formal mandate may be weak in practice, while an informal body may be influential.[46] Even if the powers of the legislature in regard to the priorities, amendment and oversight of the budget are strengthened, changes in formal rules do not necessarily translate into changes in the behaviour and attitudes of members and officials.

A radical transformation in political culture is required. First, there must be a common understanding between the executive and the legislature on the latter's constitutionally mandated oversight role. In practice, legislatures have tended to define their oversight responsibility narrowly, confining it to generating legislation rather than implementation. Members and committees have also tended to be reactive in their oversight role. On the other hand, cabinet members and MECs may see legislative oversight as intrusive and as undermining their authority. While some MECs are dissatisfied with the superficial status quo, this attitude is by no means universal (Murray and Nizjink, 2002). Saki Macozoma has described the prevailing ethos of the National Assembly as follows:

> ... the executive and the bureaucracy have not yet fully embraced the new paradigm of effective parliamentary supervision that incorporates significant public participation. This disjuncture between what Parliament wants done and what the executive and the bureaucracy are willing to do has generated considerable tensions between certain portfolio committees and departments they are supposed to oversee. [Fortunately] in the majority of cases, such tensions have resulted in departments being forced to take on broad issues raised by the portfolio committee (Sennay and Besdziek, 1999).

It may be difficult to build an institutional identity that transcends party lines and is grounded in the Constitution, but this is crucial to effective oversight. If the legislature fails to ensure that budgets reflect the electorate's priorities in regard to spending on poverty alleviation, this may increase pressure on the judiciary to intervene and evaluate service delivery in terms of progressive realisation. Concerns have been raised that a court-initiated process of setting minimum standards for service delivery in individual cases could compromise policy coherence, because of trade-offs between competing priorities. As one commentator noted:

> What if meeting the standards for socio-economic rights in the near term required punitively high levels of taxation or high levels of debt for our children to redeem? What if the standards were not set that high, but required only the resources equivalent to half the current subsidy to tertiary education and skills development? Making these decisions is inordinately complex and requires literally hundreds of officials working full-time preparing and evaluating budget

submissions. For a court to suggest that it has the wisdom to cut through these complexities and make decisions that would be in the best interest of the poor is, to say the least, an impressive leap of faith (Altbeker, 2002).

Ajam and Murray (2004) note that the judiciary has not sidestepped these issues, as shown by the Grootboom case, but has refrained from ordering the executive to reconsider public spending and from imposing a time-line for the prioritisation of socio-economic rights. They write:

> The court seems to have accepted that in providing constitutional remedies, budget impacts are inevitable. However possible budgetary impacts should be a consequence of the courts' duty to enforce progressive realisation of socio-economic rights, rather than an end in itself, which would be an unjustifiable breach of the separation of powers. The court has also avoided quantifying the precise amounts needed to be re-deployed to remedy the deviation from non-compliance with the constitution (2004).

The Treatment Action Campaign's Constitutional Court case over access to anti-retroviral treatment for pregnant mothers could have been avoided, for example, if Parliament, through its influence, had been able to bring about a higher budgetary prioritisation of HIV/AIDS – a source of concern for many citizens.[47]

A review of South Africa's electoral system, which is based solely on proportional representation at the national and provincial levels, could provide an opportunity to achieve a better balance between the need for effective oversight and other crucial objectives, such as the representation of women. Legislators who win a constituency election are less beholden to a particular party and so have more incentive to exercise oversight. Besides introducing an element of constituency-based representation, legislatures will have to consider other ways of reducing disincentives for parliamentarians to engage in oversight activities.

3.3   CAPACITY

3.3.1   INFORMATION

Supporting budget reform is one way of generating information about service delivery. For instance, section 35 of the PFMA requires the costing of legislation that has a financial impact on provinces. How many provincial NCOP delegations are mandated to request this information if it has not been provided? Committees should also demand strategic plans that are aligned with budget allocations, regular performance reports and annual reports. In-year monitoring, rather than oversight after the event, which is of limited value, can provide a means of proactive oversight and rapid remedial response.

Legislatures and committees should define their minimum information needs to avoid information overload. Performance-related information must be distributed across committees and not just in the finance committee.

Information provided by the executive may not support meaningful analysis of public expenditure, for example in relation to the impact on poverty. But unless the legislature has defined and articulated its needs – for example, which elements are required for oversight and at what level of aggregation and detail – it is difficult for the executive to respond.

The evaluation of programmes and reviews of efficiency can be an important tool for legislative oversight. However, it is highly unlikely a legislature will have sufficient time or resources to evaluate all major areas of executive activity. In these circumstances, it should focus on a limited number of high-priority projects that receive adequate planning, time and funding. To ensure that evaluations have an impact and a focus on poverty alleviation, leadership is a required. To focus its efforts, the legislature needs clearly to frame a number of questions that will facilitate evaluation, and be aware of the resources required to answer these credibly. Parliament and legislatures can also assist by embedding systematic monitoring and evaluation in departments and other organs of state by holding them accountable for implanting the strategies required by the Government-Wide Monitory and Evaluation Policy Framework (Presidency, 2007).

Furthermore, the 2009 Money Amendment Procedure and Related Matters Act calls for the establishment of a parliamentary budget office, a potentially important instrument for ensuring that the unique information needs of legislatures are met. These encompass the analysis of the technical and policy components of fiscal decision-making and the political consequences, opportunities and risks that are expected. To be effective, the budget office should be appropriately resourced, and have access to necessary economic expertise and public finance management skills. Chapter 4 discusses these questions in more detail.

Legislatures should also try to enhance the capacity for policy analysis by seeking quality information, for example, from universities, civil society and chambers of business. For this, internet access is a prerequisite.

3.3.2   COMMITTEE STRUCTURES AND PROCEDURES

Internationally, committees tend to function well in technical areas, concentrating on policy implementation rather than development. They can establish whether programmes have indeed been delivered effectively, efficiently and economically. In South Africa, performance oversight varies across committees and provinces.

Committee reports are often not debated in plenary, because of perceptions that this will duplicate work already done in party caucuses and committees. As Murray and Nijzink point out:

Plenary decisions are not regarded as adding anything substantial because party positions are unlikely to change after decisions are already taken in the caucuses where members of the executive participate. However, unless members of the legislature start to claim recognition of their separate oversight responsibility and a degree of independence with regard to the findings of committee reports, debates in plenary will not fulfil the important role of developing a democratic culture of open discussion and appraisal of performance... MPs and MPLs themselves must recognise the importance of publicly explaining the positions they take and the work they do in committee meetings (2002: 96).

In Germany, opposition party members often co-chair important committees such as the budget committee (Krafchik and Wehner, 1998). This approach could promote increasingly active oversight, particularly in public accounts committees. Alternatively, increased recognition of the need for active oversight in the ruling party could bolster the political will to hold the executive to account.

As discussed above, the strategic direction of Parliament's institutional oversight may influence the relationship between the finance committee, the public accounts committee and sector portfolio committees. The division of labour may also be affected by the amount of information submitted to Parliament, and the need to process this quickly. With the increased auditing of non-financial performance information by the Auditor-General, it is important for sector committees to engage more intensively on annual reports. Similarly, the 2007 Government-Wide Monitory and Evaluation Policy Framework requires public institutions to link a monitoring and evaluation strategy to their strategic and operational plans. There is an argument for including this in the oversight responsibilities of sector portfolio committees.

3.3.3   INTERGOVERNMENTAL AND INTERSECTORAL CO-ORDINATION

If national and provincial governments are committed to poverty eradication, they must forge closer working relations with local governments. Committees can foster this in their oversight work. For example, if a provincial department proposes new infrastructure development, such as the building of schools or clinics, committees can ensure that this is related to municipal integrated development plans.

South Africa's complex intergovernmental fiscal structure, which spans three spheres of government, public entities and other organs of state, make evaluating impacts extremely complicated. A sectoral oversight approach is required to ensure that the service delivery outputs of organs of state achieve the desired policy outcomes. Here, portfolio, budget and public accounts committees need a clear division of labour and close coordination to ensure that plans and budgets are aligned, and that implementation is subject to effective oversight.

As noted earlier, Parliament and provincial legislatures should be closely coordinated. Provincial legislatures could, for example, focus on the accountability of provincial accounting officers and MECs, as well as on the collective achievement of desired outcomes relative to provincial growth and development strategies. The National Assembly could focus on the accountability of accounting officers in national department and ministers, as well as public entities. The NCOP could monitor intergovernmental allocations, as well as the outcomes in individual sectors – for example, health, education and social development – relative to the Bill of Rights, across all spheres of government and public entities.

3.3.4   TECHNICAL SKILLS

Murray and Nijzink (2002: 90) pointed out that in a legislative landscape study some years ago that few of the respondents knew that they had the power to demand the presence of a minister or MEC "when oversight processes uncovered bad practices". Another example of the confusion about oversight powers and procedures lies in the area of political versus managerial accountability. As Murray and Nijzink note:

> In many legislatures, it is the departmental accounting officer and other officials who the politicians seek to hold accountable, rather than the responsible Minister or MEC. This misunderstanding is widespread and undermines the ability of the legislature to ensure proper political accountability. It appears to stem from a misreading of the Public Finance Management Act 1 of 1999 (2002: 89).

Even when information on the performance of a department is available, parliamentary representatives may lack the technical skills for detailed analysis and interpretation. Parliamentarians need to be trained in the more technical aspects of fiscal oversight, and training should not be confined to members of the finance and public accounts committees. If parliamentarians find dealing with input-based budgets confusing, they are unlikely to find performance budgets easier to understand unless they receive the relevant training. Organisations such as the Association of Public Accounts Committees have engaged in some concerted, institutionalised capacity-building, but these initiatives should be broadened and regularised. The latest public sector reforms emphasise monitoring and evaluation as one of the next phases, and training will be required to ensure that committee members can interpret and analyse the findings of the monitoring and evaluation of departments and public sector institutions.

Parliament and the legislatures will also have to deepen the analytical skills of their researchers so that they can engage with the continuous and growing stream of service delivery and budget information they receive, and make sensible pro-poor recommendations. Again, the proposed parliamentary budget office could become a cornerstone of effective legislative oversight, provided that it is able to attract and retain the requisite skills in budget and financial management analysis, intergovernmental fiscal relations, sector policy and implementation, quantitative methods and monitoring and evaluation. Parliament can also continue drawing on specialist institutions such as the Financial and Fiscal Commission.

4. CONCLUSION

Over time, the understanding and measurement of poverty have become more nuanced. Once seen as mainly the result of low income and a consequent lack of command over basic goods and services, definitions have increasingly expanded to include other aspects of living standards, such as health status, literacy and longevity. Most recently, appreciation of the reality of poverty has encompassed concerns about the volatility and risk of incomes, that are manifested in feelings of vulnerability. Poverty is not just "the state of having little, but also being vulnerable to lose the little one has" (Kanbur and Squire, 1999: 16). This is often associated with a lack of "voice" and political rights. With this multi-dimensional approach to poverty comes the realisation that a number of related and mutually reinforcing strategies are needed to combat it. These include the provision of basic services and infrastructure, redistribution through growth, and promoting participatory processes in all spheres of government.

Parliament and the provincial legislatures could play an important role in realising South Africa's desire to eradicate poverty in all its forms, in achieving the vision of "a better life for all" within available resources, and in ensuring that policy is translated into service delivery which has a beneficial impact on marginalised communities. Oversight is crucial because, as Schick (2002) points out: "A legislature which rewards or ignores poor results will get poor results." Systematic under-spending, revenue over-recoveries and budget surpluses clearly indicate that absolute fiscal constraints are not South Africa's major challenge, in contrast with many other developing countries (Ajam and Aron, 2007). Our malaise lies in managerial and other forms of institutional weakness. The remedy lies in the realm of institutional and management development. Parliament and the legislatures can play a crucial role in ensuring that capacity is built for poverty reduction, infrastructure and other facilitators of economic growth.

A complex interplay of factors influences the development of legislatures. They tend to evolve over time rather than being consciously designed. As one analyst has noted:

> The reality is that legislatures are not designed, with the important exception of their constitutional fundamentals. Instead, legislatures evolve organically as the many contending forces in society seek to change legislative powers, resources, internal structures and decision-making procedures (Meyers, 2000: 3).

Yet South Africa's Parliament and provincial legislatures have to make strategic choices that require stakeholders to transcend party politics in the interests of long-term institution-building, and think beyond the immediate circumstances. Legislative institutions need a vision of how to fulfil their constitutional mandates in a way that responds to current conditions, and should avoid allowing the status quo to predetermine their evolutionary path.

The challenges and intricacies are many, but if legislatures do not take the initiative at this point, they may be overtaken by external events, such as the increased use of the courts to enforce socio-economic rights. The status quo will become the default, gradually "cast in stone" as informal conventions of parliamentary impotence become entrenched. Their current capacity should not determine their long-term strategic role in fiscal oversight. However, it is crucial in rolling out a phased implementation plan to reach that destination.

The first requirement is the political will to create a legislative and executive culture of constructive fiscal oversight, and the associated enabling legislation. The creation of an institutional identity for Parliament and the legislatures is pivotal. This may also have to be fortified by other changes, such as adaptations of the electoral system, as well as capacity-building initiatives. Like all reforms, it will have to overcome internal inertia and avoid institutional backsliding. Failure to undertake it, however, will be a lost opportunity for good governance in the cause of pro-poor service delivery. For the legislatures, it may also precipitate a gradual descent into chaotic reactionary responses and eventual policy and popular irrelevance.

REFERENCES

Ajam, T. and Aron, J., " Fiscal Rennaissance in a Democratic South Afica, *Journal of Africa Economies*, 23 August 2007, http://jae.oxfordjournals.org, doi: 10.1093/jae/ejm014

Ajam, T. and C. Murray, "The Courts, Socio-economic Rights and Intergovernmental Fiscal Relations", paper presented at the Financial and Fiscal Commission 10th Anniversary Conference, "Consolidation for Equity", Cape Town, 12-14 August 2004.

Altbeker, A., "Revisiting socio-economic rights", *Business Day*, 20 May 2002.

Congress of South African Trade Unions (Cosatu), submission on the Money Bills Amendment Procedures Bill to the portfolio committee on finance, 22 October 1998. Available at: http://www.cosatu.org.za/docs/budgetsbi.htm.

Corder, H; Jagwanth, S, and Soltau, F., Report on Parliamentary Oversight and Accountability, Faculty of Law, University of Cape Town, July 1999.

Fubbs, J., "Towards effective fiscal oversight on performance budgeting to achieve results: a Gauteng perspective", paper presented for a conference on "Outcomes-based Governance: Assessing the Results", University of Stellenbosch, 12-14 September 2001.

Hartley, W., "Justice slated again for underspending", *Business Day*, 8 March 2007.

I-Net Bridge, "Govt departments under fire," 11 June 2008. Available at: http://www.fin24.com/articles/default/display_article.aspx?ArticleId=1518-25-2338521.

Kanbur, R. and Squire, L., The Evolution of Thinking about Poverty, Washington, DC: World Bank, .1999.

Hubli, K.S. and A. P. Mandaville, "Parliaments and the PRSP Process", World Bank Institute, Washington, D.C., 2004. Available at: http://siteresources.worldbank.org/WBI/Resources/wbi37231HubliMandavilleweb.pdf.

Krafchik, W. and S. Robinson, *The People's Budget and the Poor*, Cape Town, Idasa, 2004.

Krafchik, W. and J. Wehner, "The role of Parliament in the budgetary process," *South African Journal of Economics* 66 (4) 1998: 512-31.

Mbeki, T., State of the Nation Address by the President of South Africa to the Joint Sitting of the Houses of Parliament, Cape Town, 8 February 2002.

Meyers, R., "Legislative budgeting in Mexico: aspirations and choices", paper prepared for the Conference on the Reform of the State: Budget and Public Spending, Mexico City, 27 January 2000.

Murray, C. and L. Nijzink, "Building Representative Democracy: South Africa's legislatures and the Constitution", Parliamentary Support Programme, Cape Town, 2002.

National Treasury, Budget Review 2004, Government Printers, Pretoria, 2004.

Overseas Development Institute (ODI), "Parliaments and development: What shapes parliamentary performance and what can donors do to enhance it", ODI Briefing Paper, 2007. Available at:
http://www.odi.org.uk/publications/briefing/bp_april07_parliaments.pdf.

Presidency, Policy Framework for the Government-wide Monitoring and Evaluation System, Government Printers, Pretoria, 2007.

Schick, A., "Can National Legislatures Regain an Effective Voice in Budget Policy?" *OECD Journal on Budgeting* 1(3): 15-42, 2002.

Sennay, C. and Besdziek, D., "Enhancing Oversight in South Africa's Provinces: Institutions and Concerns", *African Security Review*, 8(2) 1999.

United Nations Development Programme (UNDP), "Human Rights, Governance and Sustainable Human Development", UNDP Policy Paper, New York, 1998.

Chapter 4

Budget oversight and the South African budget office

Ahmed Mohamed

1. INTRODUCTION

Accountability is an essential aspect of good democratic governance and refers broadly to the inherent responsibility of governments to account for their performance and conduct. Legislatures, with formal powers of oversight, representation and legislation, are a key dimension of accountability.

The form of governance system, the way legislatures are structured, the nature of party politics and the oversight tools available to legislatures go a long way to determining the quality of oversight and accountability. However, even the best arrangements on paper will not generate improved governance outcomes if legislatures do not have the capacity to engage on a more equal footing with the executive.

Concerns about legislative capacity are perhaps particularly acute in respect of budgeting and economic matters, which tend to be the historical preserve of the executive and which require a high degree of analytical skill. In South Africa, debates about the capacity of legislatures to engage with budgeting and economic issues have acquired particular relevance since the passing of the Money Bills Amendment Procedures and Related Matters Act. In principle, this gives Parliament almost unconstrained authority to amend the budget proposed by the executive. In the absence of adequate analytical capacity, however, such authority may be exercised poorly or not at all.

The Act calls for the establishment of a parliamentary budget office, intended to give Parliament independent research support in its engagement with the executive on the budget. Much will depend on the quality of work produced by this office and how its relationships with parliamentary committees unfold. As with any institution, it will take time to function optimally. However, there is also some urgency: the 2009 medium-term budget policy statement (MTBPS) and the 2010 budget will provide the first test of how Parliament uses the powers conferred by the Act, and will set the tone for subsequent debates on amendments and relations between the legislature and the executive.

The rest of this chapter discusses aspects of parliamentary oversight before looking in more detail at budget offices in general and South Africa's proposed budget office in particular. Section 2 explores aspects of the legislative oversight function. Section 3 takes a closer look at parliamentary committees and budget offices from a general perspective. Section 4 explores the South African budget office with a particular emphasis on its potential contributions and some conditions for its effectiveness. Section 5 concludes.

2. PARLIAMENT'S OVERSIGHT ROLE

Parliaments generally perform three key functions: representation, law-making and oversight. The representation function refers to MPs' responsibility to represent the electorate, with due regard for demographic and other differences in society. As Johnson (2005:2) aptly states: "Parliaments are the branch of government closest to the people, and MPs, more than any other officials at the national level, need to be aware of the needs of constituents, and are expected to respond to those needs." The second role of the legislature relates to the making of laws and rules that govern society. These must not only establish coherence across demographic differences, but also establish consensus on such issues as policy, taxation and expenditure. Finally, the oversight function relates to the legislature's mandate to hold the executive arm of government to account by scrutinising government affairs.

The extent to which parliaments fulfill these key functions and exert power over the executive depends, in part, on the type of legislature. Johnson and Nakamura (1999) distinguish four types of legislatures: rubber-stamp legislatures, arena legislatures, transformative legislatures and emerging legislatures. Table 1 summarises the salient features of each form of legislature and indicates their information and other capacity requirements.

Table 1: Aspects of types of legislatures		
Type of legislature	Distinguishing characteristics	Capacity requirements
Transformative legislature	Both represents and shapes societal preferences; serves as an independent shaper of policies.	High
Arena legislature	Primarily a space for the articulation and discussion of societal preferences and differences.	Moderate
Emerging legislature	Emerging or moving from one legislative type to another, usually towards a more assertive role in shaping policy.	Growing
Rubber-stamp legislature	Endorses choices made elsewhere, usually by the executive.	Low
(Adapted from Johnson and Nakumara, 1999)		

It follows from this typology that legislatures that are either transformative or emerging, or are moving from a rubber-stamp or arena status towards a transformative status, will also have higher capacity requirements and more complex organisation. In regard to budgeting, the South African Parliament seems poised to move from being primarily an arena legislature to being a potentially transformative one. As discussed in some detail below, the establishment of a budget office to support committees will contribute to the institution's ability to meet the growing demands on Parliament associated with such a shift.

Parliamentary oversight can be exercised before or after policies are adopted and implemented. Prior oversight scrutinises the potential effectiveness of proposed policies, evaluating their merits, preventing governments from abusing their power, examining and assessing legislative proposals and voting to amend, approve or reject them. Follow-up oversight monitors and evaluates the implementation of government policies. Legislatures conduct oversight through several mechanisms, including committee hearings, plenary sittings and parliamentary questions.

The effectiveness of oversight depends, among other things, on the available amendment powers, the adequacy of information and the formal and informal "rules of the game" as they affect members and committee chairpersons (Loewenberg and Patterson, 1979; Frantzich, 1979; Rockman, 1984). The range of available oversight tools also plays a crucial role in ensuring effective accountability for governance and, therefore, effective democracy. A study conducted by Pelizzo and Stapenhurst (2006a) analysed data collected by the World Bank Institute and the Inter-Parliamentary Union on the number of oversight tools available to Parliaments, and related these to those countries' forms of government, income levels and levels of democracy. The Freedom House index was used to distinguish between effective democracies (which the authors call "liberal democracies"), quasi-democracies and non-democratic states. As Table 2 suggests, a wider range of oversight tools plays a positive role in enhancing the quality of democracy, measured by the political and civil liberties a country enjoys.

Table 2: Number of oversight tools by level of democracy						
Level of democracy	Number of tools				Total	Mean
	4	5	6	7		
Democracy	1	1	7	16	25	6.52
Quasi-democracy	1	4	4	4	13	5.84
Non-democracy	4	1	4	0	9	5.00
Total					47	
Source: Pelizzo and Stapenhurst (2006a)						

The formal availability of oversight tools is, of course, only one aspect of effective engagement by a legislature. An additional factor in whether a legislature makes optimal use of its available oversight tools is parliamentary capacity. It should be borne in mind that legislatures are frequently "outgunned" by executives in terms of the analytical resources at their disposal, and perhaps particularly when they engage on public finances. Indeed, a cursory glance at the history of relations between executives and legislatures suggests a decline in legislative authority in established democracies and a tendency for legislatures in emerging democracies to remain largely subordinate to the executive. More recently, however, there have been signs of increased legislative assertiveness in many governance contexts. In the South African environment, there are indications of some shifts in power since the ANC's national conference in Polokwane in 2007. However, the political will to engage assertively with the executive, including the budget, is not sufficient for improved fiscal governance. Effective legislative engagement with the budget requires political commitment to strong oversight by parliamentary committees and capacity, for which a well-resourced and managed budget office is crucial.

3. PARLIAMENTARY COMMITTEES AND BUDGET OFFICES

Parliamentary committees are vitally important to the functioning of legislatures. They have a practical rationale: the sheer volume of work that would otherwise have to be considered in full chambers. Co-operative engagement across party lines is also likely to be easier in committees than in plenary sessions. Committees also allow members to build up expertise in particular areas, which improves their oversight. Indeed, it can be argued that the power of its committees is a prime indicator of the strength of a legislature (Freiberga, 2002).

However, as noted in the previous section, for parliamentary committees to exercise effective oversight, their members must have access to research that facilitates analysis. One way of achieving this is by establishing an independent budget research office.

Budget offices date back to the Legislative Analyst's Office in California and the US Congressional Budget Office, established in 1941 and 1974 respectively. Internationally, there has also been growth in the number of independent budget offices, as more democratic governments emerged after the Cold War, boosting multi-party governance.

The rationale for establishing a budget office is to enhance Parliament's technical capacity to exercise its functions. As Johnston writes, "… a parliament's ability to exercise its representation, lawmaking and oversight functions effectively rests to some degree on its managerial and technical capacity … Most parliamentary strengthening efforts being made today focus on building parliamentary capacity – strengthening management, infrastructure and staffing … More assertive parliaments need more expert staff to meet their greater information needs, and faster, more effective and better coordinated administrative systems"(2005:9-10).

Krafchik and Wehner (2004:2) also argue that "Parliament usually does not have sufficient information or technical capacity to play an effective role in the budget process". The lack of information and technical capacity is generally more acute in Parliaments in developing and transitional economies. Rahman argues that

" … the main rationale of empowerment of parliamentary committees is the prevailing imbalance of power between the executive and legislative branches.

To cope with the demands of modernization and complexity of society, the executive branches expanded their departments and personnel. Thus the executive's possession of an expanded workforce with sophisticated technical and specialized knowledge has enabled the executive to become the dominant player in the governance system ... [in] the legislatures on the other hand, the number rarely rises. The result has been the steady decline in the ability of the legislature to fulfil its prime functions of legislation and oversight of the executive" (2005: 5).

A 2007 joint survey by the OECD, World Bank and the Collaborative Africa Budget Reform Initiative provides further evidence that countries with a presidential system of governance tend to have more established independent budget research offices than regimes with a parliamentary form of government. As shown in Figure 1 below, 77 percent of countries with parliamentary forms of government do not have independent budget research offices, in contrast with presidential regimes, where 48 percent have yet to establish budget research offices.

Figure 1: Existence of specialised budget research office, by governance system

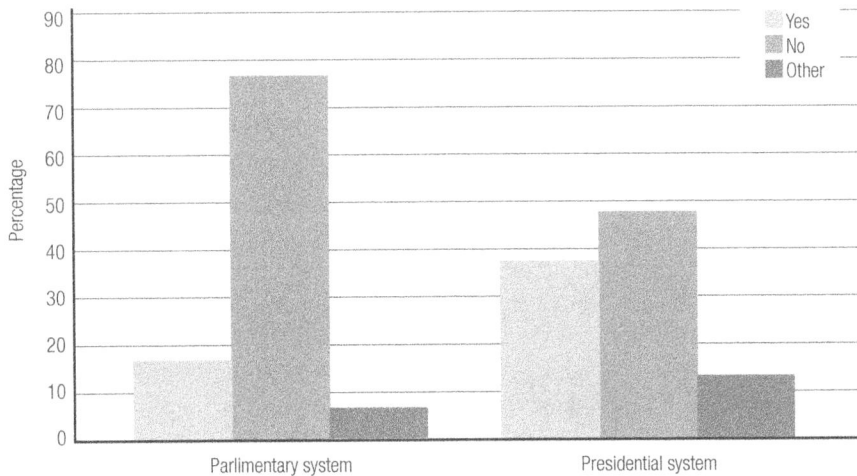

Source: OECD (2008)

These findings suggest that, when it comes to budgeting, asymmetries of power and information between the executive and legislative branches are more pronounced in parliamentary systems. This reflects their generally less assertive role and supports the earlier finding that more legislative oversight tools tend to be available in presidential and semi-presidential systems.

4. SOUTH AFRICA'S PROPOSED BUDGET OFFICE

4.1 ANALYTICAL SUPPORT

As discussed in previous chapters, the Money Bills Amendment Procedure and Related Matters Act strengthens the authority of Parliament over the budget by enabling it to amend the fiscal framework, the division of revenue, tax policy and particular appropriations. The Act sets conditions for what must be considered in amending the budget, and stipulates adherence to a particular amendment sequence.[48] However, it is fair to say that the Act does not significantly constrain Parliament's potential amendment power. Section 15 calls for the establishment of a parliamentary budget office, headed by a director. According to the legislation, the aim of the office is to provide independent, objective and professional advice and analysis to Parliament on matters related to the budget and other money bills.

The Act does not go into great detail on the content of such advice and analysis, so it is useful to give some indication of what forms of analytical support the office might regard as priorities. These might include:

4.1.1 EVALUATION OF FISCAL SUSTAINABILITY

From a macro-perspective, a "good' budget" is one whose fiscal stance makes the optimal trade-offs between the needs of the present and future generations. Put differently, government should be able to defend saving (budget surpluses) and dis-saving (budget deficits) with reference to the shorter and longer terms, and to the stability of the economy. A budget office can help to give parliamentarians a more nuanced sense of budgeting trade-offs and to assess whether the balance between sustainability and the need to do as much as possible to address existing social and economic challenges reflects the political agenda.

4.1.2 MACRO-ECONOMIC FORECASTING

There are incentives for any executive to understate and overestimate economic growth forecasts. Overestimation can occur where a government is elected on an ambitious policy platform and needs to convince the legislature and citizens that its proposals can be realised. High growth forecasts, which imply high government revenues and a larger "fiscal envelope", may make proposals appear possible when they are, in fact, unsustainable.

Underestimation can occur where there is a keen aversion to risk or where a government seeks approval for consistently collecting more revenue than planned. In recent years the South African government has often tended to underestimate revenue[49] for a given growth rate. Underestimating growth and revenue are no doubt preferable to overestimation, which may require short-term lending at less favourable interest rates. However, systematic divergences risk undermining the credibility of forecasting.

The budget office could provide independent evaluation of forecasting by identifying alternative assumptions and their implications for what has been forecast, and alert committees to consistent divergences between predictions and outcomes. The budget office neither should nor can duplicate all the complex modeling involved in the executive's forecasts. Anderson (2005, 2006) cautions against such duplication of work and suggests that the budget office should base its assessments on forecasts by private institutions, central bankers and panels of experts. It is essential to sketch alternative forecasting scenarios and insert them into the debate, and to identify systematic divergences. Such information would enable committees, including the finance committee, to engage more assertively with the executive in medium-term budget policy debates and debates on the budget itself.

4.1.3   Appropriation amendments and past performance

When they are reviewing estimates, legislature members are, or should be, interested in the outcome of ongoing programmes and the expected benefits of new programmes or changes to existing ones. The budget office must, therefore, provide appropriate evaluations on such issues. As discussed in previous chapters, the reporting requirements imposed on government departments in South Africa are fairly comprehensive and should, in principle, allow effective in-year oversight and the exercise of the power to amend budgets based on an informed sense of which departments have been performing and which have not.

Formal reporting requirements have been established and there has been some improvement in oversight by committees. But most committees remain fairly ineffective because they do not have the time or, perhaps, expertise to do the detailed work of evaluating performance in terms of departmental allocations, strategic plans, in-year spending reports, annual reports and audit results. Without such analytical findings, they have little choice but to take departmental annual reports, for example, at face value, and to ask simple clarifying questions rather than ones that genuinely probe what happened and whether the best possible outcomes were achieved. As already noted, capacity shortfalls weaken the quality of in-year oversight, while making objective amendments to appropriations on the basis of past performance virtually impossible.

4.14   NEW PROPOSALS AND CONSIDERATION OF ALTERNATIVES

Generally the executive takes the lead in drafting policy and introducing new programmes to give effect to it, with the role of the legislature being one of debate and approval. The quality of legislative debate is enhanced if committees can test new proposals against internally generated research on the cost implications and feasibility of the executive's underlying assumptions. With research at their disposal, committees would also be able to evaluate proposals against other ways of attaining the same objectives. Expecting them to conduct rigorous cost-benefit evaluations is over-ambitious, but a broad sense of costs, potential benefits and alternatives can significantly enhance the quality of debate and the reasons presented by committees for amendments. Such engagement would go a long way in developing the reputation of legislatures for being assertive, and this in turn is likely to improve the quality of arguments used by the executive in support of its proposals. In an ideal scenario, the budget office could enable committees to engage robustly with new proposals, forcing the executive to consider all possible programmes before proposing one option to a legislature.

4.1.5   LEGISLATIVE CAPACITY-BUILDING

The budget office should also continuously build the capacity of members to engage on economic and budgeting issues. As noted earlier, one of the advantages of the committee system is that it allows members to develop expertise in particular areas. This, however, will only take place if members have access to learning opportunities. Though the forms of support discussed above emphasise the technical support a budget office can provide, effective oversight does not require committees to have the same capacity as the executive. In many instances, this is unrealistic. However, members who have had the opportunity to learn are more likely to be confident in engaging the executive and asking questions that force it to clarify its assumptions and account for its achievements.

4.2   INSTITUTIONAL CONDITIONS

One must also ask what institutional conditions the budget office must meet if it is to play a meaningful role in enhancing fiscal governance. Among other things, the office should be:

4.2.1   SUFFICIENTLY CAPACITATED

The budget office should have sufficient capacity to support parliamentary committees in fulfilling their prior and follow-up oversight roles. Adequate capacity has many dimensions. Clearly, the office must be adequately financed and effectively managed. It must also build up its own working culture and institutional memory quite quickly or risk becoming irrelevant. Adequate financing will, among other things, help to ensure that the office includes a sufficient quota of analysts. South Africa, in common with many developing countries, suffers from a skills shortage, and it will be a challenge for the budget office to attract and retain sufficient analysts with expertise in the required range of disciplines.

The funding of the office should be transparent and insulated from short-term cuts. The Canadian Parliament recently proposed a 33 percent cut in the budget of its parliamentary budget office because the legislators were unhappy with its damning reports on government expenditure (May 2008). It is the democratic prerogative of any legislature to make such funding changes, but the Canadian case suggests that a transparent funding formula based on incremental adjustments should be the norm, and that any proposed cuts should meet stringent criteria that can be publicly debated.

After the 2009 elections, the South African Parliament had 39 portfolio, standing or joint committees and 10 select committees. The budget office will focus on supporting those committees that engage most directly on the budget: the finance committee and the joint budget committee on appropriation.[50] However, given that they have also been given authority to propose appropriation amendments, other committees will also need, and request, budget analysis capacity. There is a risk that the budget office's analytical services could be spread too thinly across too many committees for effective, coordinated engagement. Management of the office will have to develop a set of short-term and long-term strategic priorities in consultation with committees to minimise this risk. Individual analysts might, for example, be attached to particular committees for specified periods of the year, but work together during the key phases of budget and MTBPS debate.

4.2.2   ACCOUNTABLE AND TRANSPARENT

The budget office should, of course, account to Parliament for the quality of the analytical work it generates. One way of helping Parliament evaluate its work would be to require it to submit its outputs regularly for external peer review. Transparency in identifying research priorities and in the deployment of analysts will also foster confidence in the office. In the interests of transparency, its outputs should be publicly available.

4.2.3   INDEPENDENT AND NON-PARTISAN

In South Africa's electoral system, MPs owe their seats to their standing in their own party rather than to a constituency election. This gives a greater weight to party loyalty and cohesion than a presidential or constituency-based parliamentary system. Accordingly, there is a risk that members of the ruling party will expect the budget office to generate research results that support the proposals of the executive, with which they share political allegiance. If research by the budget office contradicts such proposals, there may be a tendency to ignore it or put pressure on the office to revaluate its findings and align them more closely with the thinking of the party and executive. The Act seeks to address this concern by emphasising the independence and non-partisanship of the office.

As discussed, the work of the office will have to be of a high academic standard and will benefit greatly from a detailed analysis of particular questions, rather than general and empirically unsubstantiated arguments. As far as possible, it must also aim to sketch alternative scenarios and interpretations by providing the facts in a politically neutral way, so that those who have a political mandate can make decisions. Analysts must feel secure they can draw the most likely conclusions from the available evidence. As regards the credibility of the office for both the ruling and opposition parties, much will depend on the stature of the director. He or she will have to be a respected analyst; should have experience in a range of working environments, including government, academia and the NGO sector; and should not be closely associated with any political party. The director's term should also be secure, with stringent and transparent conditions tied to dismissal before it expires.

5. CONCLUSION

This chapter has sketched aspects of oversight, focusing on the role a budget office can play in enhancing the capacity of legislature committees. It has pointed to possible analytical work the office could provide and to some of the conditions for it to be credible and effective. It is envisaged that many of the issues discussed here will play themselves out in South Africa, particularly over the next two or three years, and that with its newfound power to make amendments Parliament will engage on the budget for the first time. We have already alluded to some of the key challenges the office is likely to face. They can perhaps be usefully divided into political, analytical and institutional challenges.

Research priorities are never set in an entirely neutral fashion. They take their cue from the perceived priorities of the day, as reflected in the media, political debates and the political objectives of parties. To remain relevant, the budget office will have to derive its agenda from such debates and from the corresponding needs of committees and their members. However, though a parliamentary budget office is inevitably embedded in the issues and discourses of the day, this does not mean that it should not be vigilant in resisting political interference. Pressure could take the form of requiring the office to pursue research priorities that meet party political needs rather than those of Parliament and citizens, and of attempts to dismiss or sanitise reports that challenge the executive.

On the analytical challenges, it is a truism that South Africa has a shortage of top-end skills. The office could struggle to attract and retain the analytical capacity it requires, particularly analysts who can do multi-disciplinary work. Offering market-related pay is one way of recruiting skilled people, but other factors also come into play. These include the ability of staff to further develop their own expertise; to feel the work they are doing has a meaningful impact on the quality of governance; to see opportunities for career-pathing; and to be part of an institution that is highly regarded.

The institutional challenges facing the office are the familiar ones associated with any newly established institution. Under pressure from committees that have new powers and require support, it will have to establish an efficient and effective working culture and determine its priorities with an eye to their needs, the resources available to it, and the fundamental requirement that its work should be of a high technical standard.

None of these challenges is insurmountable. Furthermore, a gradualist approach may be appropriate in building analytical and institutional capacity. Krafchik and Wehner (2004: 10) argue that "the beginning need not be elaborate". As with Parliament's exercise of its budgetary amendment authority, the office would do far better to proceed carefully, with a sense of its own limitations, than to take on too much, spread itself too thinly and lose credibility, as this could be very hard to regain.

REFERENCES

Barry, A., "The value of a nonpartisan, independent, objective analytic unit to the legislative role in budget preparation", paper presented at the 2005 annual meeting of the Southern Political Science Association, New Orleans, Louisiana.

Barry, A., "The value of a nonpartisan, independent, objective analytic unit to the legislative role in budget preparation", *Sourcebook on Legislative Budget Offices*, Parliamentary Strengthening Program, World Bank Institute, Washington D.C., 2008.

Birungi, B.K., "Establishment of Uganda's parliamentary budget office and parliamentary budget committee", *Sourcebook on Legislative Budget Offices*, Parliamentary Strengthening Program, World Bank Institute, Washington D.C., 2008.

Frantzich, S.E., "Computerised Information Technology in the US House of Representatives", *Legislative Studies Quarterly*, Vol 4 (2) 1979: 255-280.

Freiberga, I., "The Role of Parliamentary Committees in Formulating Education Policy", Organisation for Economic Co-operation and Development, 2002.

Jenkins, R., "The role of political institutions in promoting accountability", in

Performance Accountability and Combating Corruption, Anwar Shah (ed.), World Bank, Washington D.C., 2007.

Johnson, J.K., "The Role of Parliament in Government", International Bank for Reconstruction and Development/The World Bank, Washington D.C., 2005.

Johnson, J.K. and R.T. Nakamura, "Concept Paper on Legislatures and Good Governance", United Nations Development Programme, 1999. Available at: http://www.undp.org/governance/docs/Parl-Pub-ConceptPaper.htm

Johnson, J.K. and R. Stapenhurst, "Strengthening Public Accounts Committees by Targeting Regional and Country-Specific Weaknesses", in *Performance Accountability and Combating Corruption*, Anwar Shah (ed.), World Bank: Washington D.C., 2007.

Johnson, J.K and R. Stapenhurst, "The growth of parliamentary budget offices", *Sourcebook on Legislative Budget Offices*, Parliamentary Strengthening Program, World Bank Institute, Washington D.C., 2008.

Krafchik, W and J. Wehner, "Legislatures and Budget Oversight: Best Practices", paper presented at the Open Forum held by Kazakhstan Revenue Watch in Almaty, April 8, 2004.

Loewenberg, G. and S.C. Patterson, *Comparing Legislatures*. Boston, Little Brown and Co., 1979.

May, K., "Embattled budget officer's funding frozen", *The Ottawa Citizen*, 2008.

OECD, Survey of budget practices and procedures in OECD countries, The 2008 World Bank/OECD survey of budget practices and procedures in Asia and other regions, and the 2008 CABRI/OECD survey of budget practices and procedures in Africa. Available online at: http://www.oecd.org/document/61/0,3343,en_2649_34119_2494461_1_1_1_1,00.html

Pelizo, R. and R. Stapenhurst, "Democracy and Oversight", in *Parliamentary Oversight for Government Accountability*, Pelizo R., R Stapenhurst and D. Olson (eds.), International Bank for Reconstruction and Development/The World Bank Institute, Washington D.C., 2006a.

Pelizo, R. and R. Stapenhurst, "Public Accounts Committees", in *Parliamentary Oversight for Government Accountability*, Pelizo, R., R. Stapenhurst and D. Olson (eds.), International Bank for Reconstruction and Development/The World Bank Institute, Washington D.C., 2006b.

Pennings, P., "Parliamentary Control of the Executive in 47 Democracies", Paper prepared for the workshop on parliamentary control of the executive, ECPR Joint Sessions of Workshops, Copenhagen, April 14-19, 2000.

Rahman, T., "Parliamentary control and government accountability in Sri Lanka: The role of parliamentary committees", Department of Public and Social Administration, City University of Hong Kong Working Paper Series, 2005.

Rockman, B.A., "Legislative-Executive Relations and Legislative Oversight", *Legislative Studies Quarterly*, Vol 9 (3) 1984: 387-440.

Shugart, M.S., "Semi-presidential system: Dual Executive and Mixed Authority Patterns", Graduate School of International Relations and Pacific Studies, University of California, San Diego, 2005.

Uhr, J. "Creating a Culture of Integrity", Commonwealth Secretariat, United Kingdom, 2003.

Verwey, L., "Revenue Estimation, the Budget Balance and Fiscal Accountability in South Africa: Some Recent Experiences", PIMS Budget Paper 1, available at www.idasa.org

Wehner, J., "Back from the Sidelines? Redefining the Contribution of Legislatures to the Budget Cycle", Working Paper Series on Contemporary Issues in Parliamentary Development, World Bank Institute, Washington D.C., 2004.

Chapter 5

Public participation in budgeting: opportunities presented by new amendment powers

Kate Lefko-Everett and Musa Zamisa

1. INTRODUCTION

Before South Africa's transition to democracy in 1994, most citizens were excluded from meaningful participation in public and representative institutions. Policy, legislative processes and decision-making in both the executive and Parliament were often archaic and secretive, serving to entrench the discrimination and inequities of the apartheid state.

During the democratic transition, the ANC-led government committed itself clearly and explicitly to a more participatory approach to governance, which would involve citizens in identifying national values and priorities, developing policy and drafting new legislation (Lefko-Everett, 2009). As a result, public participation is among the core principles enshrined in the 1996 Constitution, which prescribes public access to, and involvement, in both houses of Parliament, as well as in the public administration of all spheres of government.

Drafters of the 1996 Constitution also envisaged a deliberative and consultative national budgeting process. Section 77 prescribes the introduction of an Act of Parliament to provide a procedure for the legislature to amend money bills. These powers would allow elected representatives to deliberate on and make changes to legislation related to the appropriation of public funds, in line with policy priorities and the public interest.

Until recently, however, the budget amendment powers required by section 77 of the Constitution were among the last constitutional prescriptions not to be placed on the statute book. Parliament's ability to engage with the budget was, therefore, limited, as was the ability of the public to participate meaningfully in budget deliberations during the legislative phase (Lefko-Everett, 2008). As discussed in previous chapters, the Money Bills Amendment Procedure and Related Matters Bill [B75-2008] was introduced in Parliament in 2008 and signed into law by President Kgalema Motlanthe in April 2009, giving Parliament authority to amend budgets.

Importantly, the new Act carves out a number of dedicated spaces for public participation during the legislative phase of the budget in Parliament. This is an important development in furthering participatory governance in South Africa. But of critical importance will be the way accompanying structures and practices are established, to ensure that participation is effective and meaningful, and goes beyond the mere "cosmetic fulfilment of constitutional rights" (Seedat, 2007a).

This chapter begins with a brief overview of the framework for public participation in the legislature, followed by a discussion of participatory budgeting internationally and in South Africa. Next, we assess the extent of participation in Parliament's finance committee between 1999 and 2008. We then examine new opportunities for participation created by the Act, before turning to some of the risks and challenges of increased participation.

2. PUBLIC PARTICIPATION IN SOUTH AFRICA

Public participation is crucial in building consent, confidence and trust in the legitimacy of a democratic state. Levin (2004) writes that public participation is critical in "all phases of government programmes, from design through to implementation and evaluation", to ensure that the needs of the public are "properly articulated and addressed". In a democratic society, he suggests, the need to engage with citizens "never ends" (Levin, 2004: 28; 31).

With South Africa's transition to democracy in 1994 came a commitment to a more inclusive and participatory form of governance. Accordingly, public participation is among the central values enshrined in the 1996 Constitution, which provides for the involvement of citizens in both houses of Parliament and all spheres of public administration.

Sections 59 and 72 of the Constitution require that both the National Assembly and the National Council of Provinces (NCOP) "facilitate public involvement" in legislative and other processes. Both are also required to conduct their business in an "open manner". Sittings of the National Assembly, NCOP and committees of both houses must be accessible and open to the public, with access regulated only when it is reasonable and justifiable in an open and democratic society. The right of the public to "actively and meaningfully participate in legislative processes" has been upheld in a number of Constitutional Court rulings in recent years (Seedat, 2007a). Section 195 of the Constitution also requires that in the public administration, all spheres of government, organs of state and public enterprises, "people's needs must be responded to, and the public must be encouraged to participate in decision-making".

The public can take part in Parliament's legislative processes in a number of ways. Most meetings of parliamentary portfolio committees and sittings of the National Assembly are open to the public. Parliament also convenes public hearings on specific themes, including policy issues and draft legislation (De Villiers, 2001). The rules of Parliament also allow citizens to raise concerns about existing legislation by means of petitions. Any member of the public who wishes to petition the legislature must approach an MP, who "must lodge the petition with the Secretary. The Secretary must submit the petition to the Speaker for approval. If approved, the Speaker must table the petition in the Assembly" (De Villiers, 2001).

However, the right to petition Parliament has not been used frequently, and appears to involve a lengthy process. To cite a recent example, it was only in 2006 that Parliament acceded to a petition brought to Parliament by Chloë Kellerman two years earlier over a dispute with the Government Employees Pension Fund. Kellerman then waited until 2008 for a money bill to be introduced to allow for the transfer of the pension sum (Parliamentary Monitoring Group, 2005; SABiNet, 2008). It is far more common for members of the public to make submissions to Parliament on policy, draft legislation and other topical issues, as shown by the case study on the finance committee later in this chapter. Submissions may be made in writing or orally, at public hearings or directly to portfolio committees.

However, the relatively strong legal and procedural framework for public participation in Parliament has not always guaranteed a high standard of participation, or ensured that public input is meaningfully incorporated into decision-making. Critics suggest that, in reality, public participation often fails to extend beyond a "formality used merely to further an existing government agenda" (Seedat, 2007a).

Disregard for the principle of public participation and the value of citizens' input into governance was highlighted by comments last year by ANC MP Maggie Sotyu, chairperson of Parliament's safety and security committee. Before the start of public hearings on the proposed incorporation of the Directorate of Special Operations ("Scorpions") into the South African Police Service – among the most protracted and contested public hearings in Parliament in recent years – Sotyu presented the incorporation of the Scorpions as a *fait accompli* to the media, stating: "The Scorpions are going to be dissolved. Our (role) as parliament is to implement the policies of the ruling party." (De Lange, 2008: 2)

The recently released Report of the Independent Panel Assessment of Parliament also documents a number of obstacles that have hindered meaningful public participation in Parliament. These include the costs of engaging with Parliament, language barriers, limited advertising of public hearings, and minimal feedback after most public participation processes (Independent Panel Assessment of Parliament, 2009: 54-55). However, the report also calls on Parliament to become the "premier forum for the public consideration of issues" in keeping with its constitutional mandate, and to uphold its vision as an institution that is "responsive to the needs of the people and that is driven by the ideal of realising a better quality of life for all the people of South Africa." (2009: 47)

3. PARTICIPATION IN BUDGETING

In South Africa and elsewhere, the national budget is a crucial policy instrument and a central pillar of governance. The budget encompasses government's economic policy priorities, macro-economic position, revenue intake and all appropriations of public funds. Virtually every policy decision made in government has budgetary implications, and in a democracy it is crucial that budgeting is transparent, accountable and open to public input and scrutiny. It is, as Krafchik writes, the "government's most important economic policy instrument", and provides a "comprehensive statement of the nation's priorities" (Krafchik, 2001: 105).

In many countries, citizens have tended to be excluded from participation in budget processes. Bräutigam suggests that this was particularly common in the 1990s, when the "reigning assumption among academics and many development policy advisers was that macroeconomic policy-making, and indeed, many areas of revenue and expenditure management, needed to be somewhat exclusionary in order to allow technical consideration, and not 'politics' to dominate" (Bräutigam, 2004: 4). However, World Bank research has found a link between greater public participation in policy formulation and implementation and "two elements found to be associated with successful management of economic policy: ownership and credibility" (Johnson and Wasty, 1993, in Bräutigam, 2004: 4-5). In Latin America and Europe, in particular, participatory budgeting practices have been introduced in which citizens take on an active role in deliberating and negotiating over the distribution of public resources and deciding how and where public resources should be spent.

In addition to increasing "ownership and credibility", a participatory approach has also been shown to improve the developmental and policy outcomes of the budget. Public participation has the potential to increase the allocative efficiency of the budget and generate a closer alignment between the preferences of citizens and the way in which public funds are allocated and spent by government. It also provides strong support for improved operational efficiency, by encouraging greater awareness of budgetary policy and allocations and increased public scrutiny of implementation.

One successful example of this, documented by the International Budget Partnership, is that of Mexican research and advocacy organisation Fundar. In 2005, Fundar identified an unprecedented and disproportionate budgetary allocation to the Seguro Popular healthcare programme, far exceeding funding to other institutions and programmes, including the National HIV/AIDS Centre. After monitoring HIV/AIDS budgets through Mexico's Federal Institute of Access to Public Information, it concluded there had been low levels of information from government agencies, contradictory responses from various institutions, a lack of accountability, and unclear discretion over the use of HIV/AIDS funds, among other shortcomings. Alarmingly, it also found that institutions specialising in HIV/AIDS treatment did not receive priority treatment in the budget, fuelling suspicions of mismanagement and the misallocation of funds and potentially detracting from the effectiveness of the country's HIV/AIDS response. Fundar's subsequent advocacy strategy led to a major budgetary turnabout by the House of Representatives in 2006, which saw considerable increases in budgets of HIV/AIDS-related programmes and institutions (Ramkumar, 2008: 41-43).

South Africa has made significant strides in developing an open and transparent budget process in its first 15 years of democracy. In 2008, the International Budget Partnership's Open Budget Index ranked South Africa among the five countries with the most transparent budgeting systems of 85 surveyed worldwide, alongside the United Kingdom, France, New Zealand and the United States.

Nonetheless, in spite of the constitutional framework discussed above, public participation in budgeting has traditionally remained quite limited. The drafting of the budget, including debate and decisions on the fiscal framework, division of revenue and particular allocations, takes place largely in the executive, in forums such the minister's committee on the budget and the budget council (National Treasury,

2007). Krafchik confirms that opportunities for participating in or influencing the South African budget in the drafting stage are "informal and require direct engagement with line departments in national and provincial government". These opportunities, he suggests, often "depend on personal contact and a history of budget policy involvement" (Krafchik, 2001: 94).

For this reason, opportunities for public participation in the legislative phase of the budget are particularly important, for example by means of submissions and presentations to portfolio committees. Krafchik suggests that Parliament is the most appropriate body to "ensure that the budget best matches the nation's needs with the available resources", and that the legislative phase should provide the "most significant opportunity for the public and civil society to voice their preferences and commit themselves to the choices made" (Krafchik, 2001: 105).

As discussed in the next section, a wide range of actors participates in the activities of Parliament, and specifically in budget processes. However, until recently, the lack of budgetary amendment powers prevented elected officials and members of the public from playing as active a role in budgeting as initially envisaged. The lack of such powers was a source of frustration for many, and civil society organisations in particular. For example, in 1998 the then deputy secretary-general of the Congress of South African Trade Unions (Cosatu), Zwelinzima Vavi, commented that the organisation had continually made "detailed submissions to the standing committee on public finance, calling on them to initiate legislation to empower Parliament to oversee government spending and priorities in line with the constitution". Vavi said that Cosatu was "tired of making the same points to the standing committee on public finance year after year". He also warned that "unless assured otherwise, we have no intention of making yet another submission just for the sake of being counted amongst those that have spoken, when our recommendations are ignored" (Vavi, 1998).

Similarly, the People's Budget Campaign (PBC), which represents a number of civil society organisations, stopped making submissions to Parliament on the annual budget. Responding to an invitation from the finance committee to make an input into the deliberations on the 2006/07 budget, the campaign stated:

> We have consistently campaigned for the full implementation of section 77 of the Constitution through the enactment of legislation to permit Parliament, as the primary forum for popular engagement with government policy, to amend money bills, including the national budget. Until Parliament is equipped with meaningful money bill amendment powers, it will remain unable to give effect to any changes proposed by the PBC or other civil society organisations. (Cosatu, 2006.)

The sense among citizens' groups and civil society organisations that they cannot participate in governance or effect meaningful change is undesirable in a democratic state, and affects perceptions of government transparency and legitimacy. This is of particular concern in the current political climate, in which the Public Service Commission suggests that "public confidence in the country's institutions and leaders has dropped" (PSC, 2008: 14; Friedman, 2006). The commission also suggests that in South Africa, "ours is a citizenry that not only values but also expects public participation", and warns that "if state institutions do not institutionalise and adequately promote public participations, citizens are likely to find other ways to express themselves and attract attention, even if this involves using less constructive mechanisms" (PSC, 2008: 139).

4. Case study: Portfolio committee on finance

Given the importance of public participation in South Africa, and the obstacles to participation in the budgeting process, it is important to examine the extent of current participation in Parliament, particularly in the budget process. With this in mind, a case study of the finance committee was conducted with the aim of determining whether opportunities exist in Parliament for participation in matters related to public finances; the extent to which these opportunities are used by organisations and members of the public; and whether substantive participation has occurred around the annual budget, even in the absence of amendment powers.

For this analysis, we chose Parliament's finance committee because it considers both the budget and the medium-term budget policy statement (MTBPS), as well as processing finance-related legislation and conducting oversight of the finance ministry and related departments. Committee reports captured and published online by the non-governmental Parliamentary Monitoring Group (PMG) were used as a data source.[51] PMG reports were analysed over a 10-year period, from 1999-2008 (see PMG online).

The records suggest that the finance committee meets, on average, about 54 times a year. Over the 10-year period, the committee met most frequently in 2001 (79 times), and least often in 1999 (26 times). On average, opportunities for active public participation, beyond attending meetings, featured in about 16 meetings every year, or 30 percent, as shown in Figure 1 on the following page.

Between 1999 and 2008, about 618 submissions were made to the committee, at an average of 62 submissions a year. The highest number of submissions was made in 2004 (45), most of which (29) were in response to the Financial Services Laws General Amendment Bill.

Figure 1: Public participation in finance committee meetings

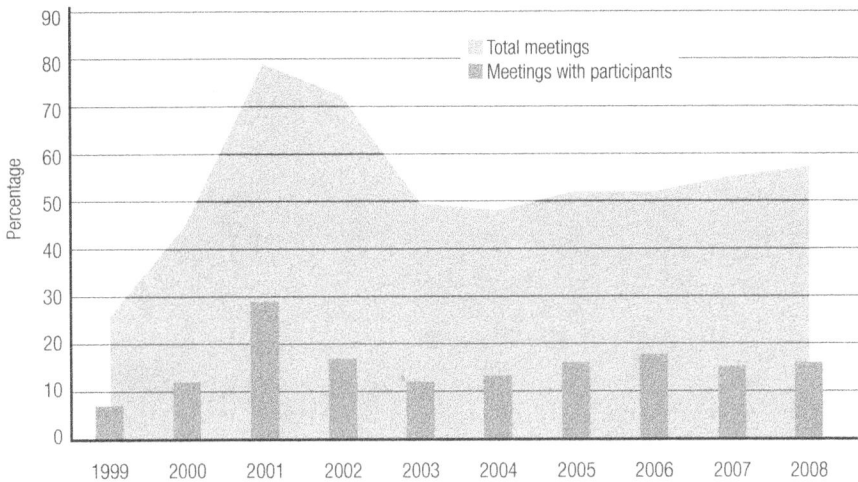

The 618 submissions received by the committee came from some 276 sources. For the purpose of analysis, the sources were grouped into the following nine categories:

- academic institutions/staff, and affiliated research units (23);
- businesses/private sector (74);
- industrial bodies and professional/sector associations[52] (59);
- constitutional or other independent bodies (7);
- government (28);
- individuals making independent submissions (34);
- unions and organised labour (7);
- non-governmental and community-based organisations (35); and
- political parties and affiliated organisations (9).

Using these categories, our analysis indicates that, broadly speaking, submissions to the finance committee over the 10-year period have been dominated by industrial bodies, professional/sector associations and the private sector. Figure 2 on the following page shows that in eight out of the 10 years analysed, the largest numbers of submissions have come from industrial bodies and professional/sector associations.

The only exceptions were in 1999, when non-governmental and community-based organisations made a large number of submissions in response to the Katz Commission Report on Fiscal Issues Affecting Non-Profit Organisations (13), and in 2002, when the majority of submissions came from government departments in response to the Municipal Finance Management Bill (24). In 2003 and 2006, the number of submissions made by industrial bodies and professional or sector associations was also matched by submissions by the private sector.

Figure 2: Source of submissions as a share of total, 1999-2008

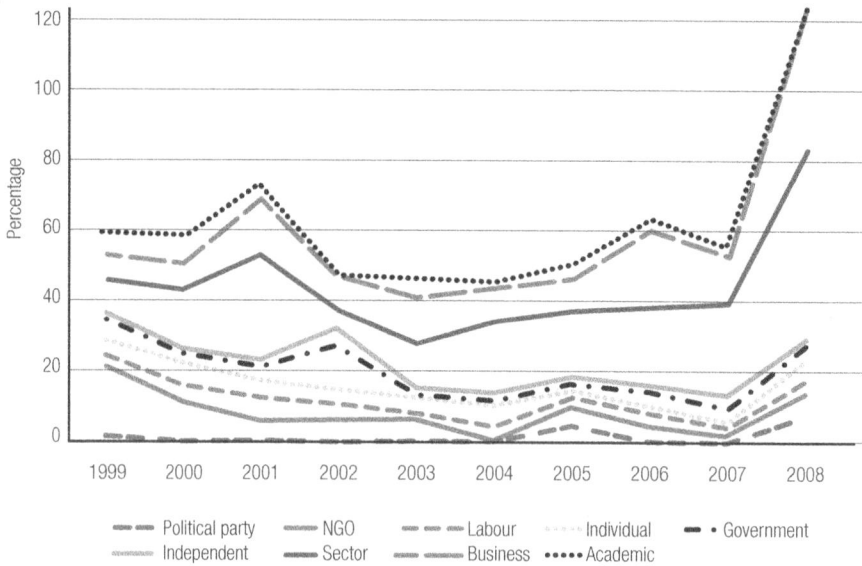

Interestingly, 196 of the 618 submissions made to the finance committee, or 32 percent, came from only 11 sources. Most submissions overall were made by the South African Institute of Chartered Accountants (Saica) (27) and the South African Banking Association (previously the Banking Council) (25, plus one joint submission).

In all, five of these sources were industrial bodies and professional/sector associations: Saica, the South African Banking Association, the South African Chamber of Business (Sacob) (20), Life Offices Association (18) and Business Unity South Africa (Busa) (17). Other organisations that made relatively large numbers of submissions to the committee over the 10 years were Cosatu (18), Price Waterhouse Coopers (17), the Federation of Unions of South Africa (Fedusa) (17), the Financial and Fiscal Commission (13), Idasa (13) and Standard Bank (10). (See Figure 3 on the following page.)

In addition to sources, we analysed the subjects of submissions to the finance committee. Over the 10 years, submissions were made on some 53 wide-ranging topics, including draft legislation, the budget and the MTBPS, as well specific issues for debate such as monetary policy, sector contributions to the economy, taxation, access to finance and the insurance industry. Notably, between 1999 and 2008, the largest number of submissions was received in response to the annual budget (95), despite Parliament's lack of amendment powers. This was closely followed by submissions on the Revenue Laws Amendment Bill (93) and Taxation Laws Amendment Bill (41).

However, while cumulatively the highest numbers of overall submissions focused on the annual budget and Revenue Laws Amendment Bills tabled each year, analysis also shows that in particular years, other topics drew as many or more submissions. Table 1 on the following page shows the topics on which the highest and second highest numbers of submissions were received each year.

Figure 3: Contribution of submissions from 11 main sources

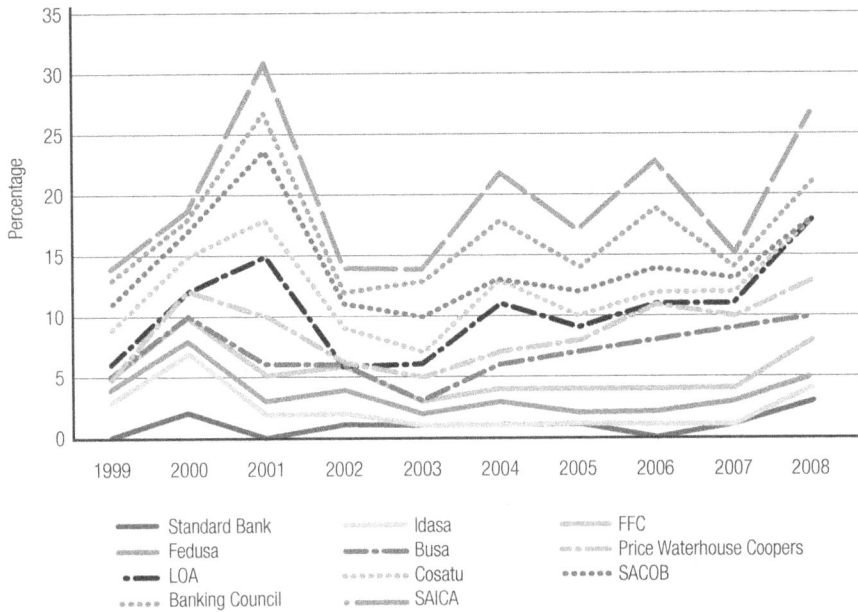

Table 1: Topics generating the highest number of submissions		
	Highest number of submissions	Second highest number of submissions
1999	Katz Commission Report: Land Reform Tax (15)	Katz Commission Report: Fiscal Issues Affecting NPOs (13)
2000	Budget 2000 (14)	Revenue Issues and Tax Proposals (10)
2001	Budget 2001 (14)	Financial Intelligence Centre Amendment Bill (11)
2002	Municipal Finance Management Bill (24)	Budget 2002 (10)
2003	Revenue Laws Amendment Bill (11)	Exchange Control Amnesty and Amendment of Taxation Laws Bill (10)
2004	Revenue Laws Amendment Bill (10)	Budget 2004 (9)
2005	Budget 2005 (9) and Revenue Laws Amendment Bill (9)	Bills of Exchange Amendment Bill (7)
2006	SARS discussion paper on tax avoidance (14)	Bulking in the Insurance Industry (12)
2007	Pension Funds Amendment Bill (12)	Revenue Laws Amendment Bill (9)
2008	Financial Services Laws General Amendment Bill (29)	Financial Intelligence Centre Amendment Bill (16)

Finally, our analysis focused on submissions made specifically on the budget each year. Over the 10-year period, 95 submissions were made on the budget, or 15% of all submissions received. This proportion is relatively small, but again, the budget received more submissions than any other topic, and this is significant given that the lack of amendment powers precluded any changes in response to public input.

As with other topics, the majority of submissions on the budget were made by the private sector (24) and industrial bodies and professional/sector associations (22). Submissions by these two categories cumulatively accounted for 48% of all budget submissions. Submissions by other categories of sources are shown in Figure 4.

However, a closer look at sources shows that the labour union, Fedusa, in fact made the highest number of submissions on the budget from a single source: one every year, or 10 in total. Other sources making relatively high numbers of submissions over the 10-year period were: Busa (six, including three joint submissions), Sacob (five, including one joint submission), the Chamber of Commerce and Industry South Africa (Chamsa) (five, including three joint submissions), Idasa (five), Standard Bank (five) and the Black Business Council (four).

Figure 4: Total budget submissions by source

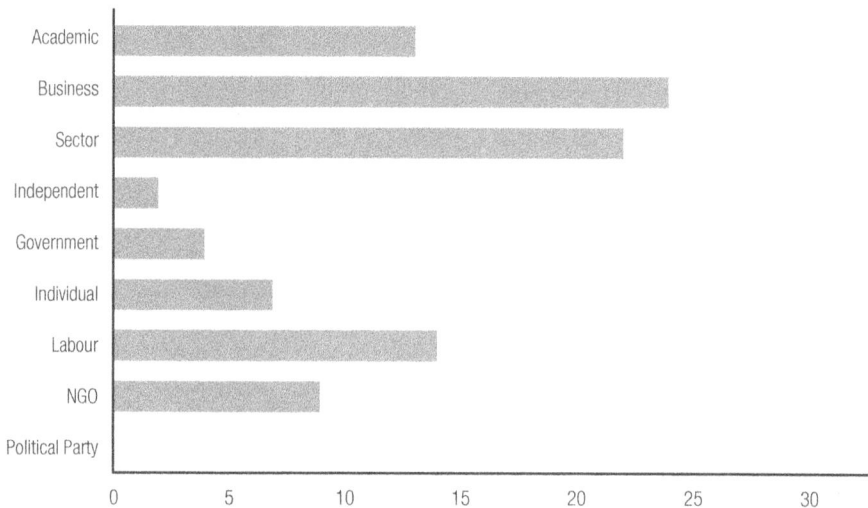

A number of interesting findings emerge from this analysis. In the first instance, about one in three meetings of the finance committee, on average, features public participation. Compared with other committees, this is a fairly high proportion, considering the substantial work that the committee does in developing draft legislation and carrying out its oversight function.

At the same time, it is difficult to assess the quality of this public participation and the extent to which the committee takes into account the input it receives. On some occasions, it appears that reports are written summarising inputs and proposals by the public. At face value, this is an important indicator that public inputs have been documented and considered. However, reporting on public participation appears to be inconsistent, and there is scope for improvement.

As discussed, the private sector and bodies or associations that represent sector-specific interests have dominated public participation in the finance committee. Of course, to some extent this is to be expected, given that policy and legislation regulating the private sector and finance industry fall within the committee's remit. However, it is also clear that these organisations are particularly vigilant about following the work of Parliament, and have the capacity and resources to engage with the committee when the opportunity arises, irrespective of budgetary amendment powers.

Analysis also suggests that submissions from academia, non-governmental organisations and community-based organisations, and members of the public are often sporadic and outnumbered. Certainly, civil society should actively use available channels of participation that private interests consistently use. However, as the Report of the Independent Panel Assessment of Parliament acknowledges, it is also Parliament's responsibility to pursue balanced and diverse public input and overcome persistent obstacles to participation, including language barriers and unaffordable costs for the poor (Independent Panel Assessment of Parliament, 2009: 54-55).

Finally, it was interesting to note that while the budget consistently draws a relatively large share of submissions every year, the same is not true of the MTBPS. In fact, only 27 submissions on the MTBPS were recorded over the 10-year period.

The MTBPS is an important medium-term policy statement that sets out national economic policy priorities, responses to economic trends, revenue forecasts and adjustments to spending priorities for the coming three fiscal years (Verwey and Lefko-Everett, 2007: 3-4). There is certainly room for Parliament to broaden participation at this point in the budget process, and research suggests this could increase "ownership and credibility" of economic policy (Johnson and Wasty, 1993, in Bräutigam, 2004: 4-5).

5. New opportunities for participation created by the Act

Our analysis of public participation in the finance committee leads to a number of important conclusions. Firstly, the level of participation in committees appears to be fairly high, although again, this is not necessarily an indicator of the quality of participation. Secondly, even without amendment powers, there have been submissions on the budget each year. Thirdly, public participation has been dominated by industrial bodies and professional/sector associations, and the private sector.

However, the introduction of the Money Bills Amendment Procedure and Related Matters Bill, and its recent signing into law, suggests that the nature of public participation in budgeting in South Africa is set to change. Importantly, the new Act creates a number of dedicated avenues for public participation in the budget process.

One of the central features of the Act is likely to result in a change in the structure of committees. Two committees have dominated examination of the budget:

the finance committee and the joint budget committee (JBC). As discussed above, the finance committee mainly processed legislation and conducted oversight, while the JBC focused on analysing proposed allocations in the medium-term expenditure framework and Appropriation Bill, ensuring that these were consistent with constitutional mandates and government policy. The JBC also monitored departmental revenue and expenditure and examined the MTBPS, with the exception of aspects related to the macro-economy and revenue (Parliament of South Africa online).

The new Act requires each house of Parliament to establish a committee on finance and a separate committee on appropriations, and the JBC has been recast as the joint budget committee on appropriation.

In the structure envisaged by the Act, the new finance committee will consider such issues as "the national macroeconomic and fiscal policy; amendments to the fiscal framework; revised fiscal framework and revenue proposals and Bills; actual revenue published by the National Treasury; and any other related matter" set out in the Act (Sec 4 (2)).

For its part, the JBC on appropriation will focus on "spending issues; amendments to the Division of Revenue Bill, the Appropriation Bill, Supplementary Appropriations Bills and the Adjustment Appropriations Bill; recommendations of the Financial and Fiscal Commission, including those referred to in the Intergovernmental Fiscal Relations Act, 1997 (Act No. 97 of 1997); reports on the actual expenditure published by the National Treasury; and any other related matter" set out in the Act (Sec 4 (3)).

Importantly, the Act creates a number of dedicated avenues for public participation, both in committees and during various phases of the budget. The first opportunity for participation is on the fiscal framework, which provides estimates of aggregate revenue, expenditure, borrowing, debt servicing costs and the contingency reserve for the year. The Act stipulates that when the budget is tabled, the National Assembly and the NCOP must refer the fiscal framework and revenue proposals to their respective finance committees. Section 8 (2) specifies that these "must conduct joint public hearings on the fiscal framework and revenue proposals".

Once the fiscal framework has been adopted, the Division of Revenue Bill and Appropriation Bill must be referred to the appropriation committee. The standing rules must provide for public hearings in respect of the passing of both bills. All revenue bills must also be referred to the National Assembly's finance committee and again, the standing rules must provide for public hearings on them.

Finally, all other money bills before Parliament must be referred to the appropriations committee, which must conduct public hearings. Sections of the Act that provide for public participation are shown in Table 2 on the following page.

The Act's inclusion of these opportunities for public participation is an important step towards a more participatory approach to budgeting in South Africa. For citizens and civil society and other organisations, the prospect of making a real contribution to budgeting through new amendment powers is a welcome development. However, the ways in which these opportunities are used will be critical.

Table 2: Public participation requirements in the 2009 Act		
Section	Topic	Public hearings
8 (2)	Fiscal framework & revenue proposals	NA & NCOP finance committees
9 (5)	Division of Revenue bill	NA appropriations committee
10 (8)	Appropriation bill	NA appropriations committee
11 (4)	Revenue bill	NA finance committee
13	Other money bills	NA appropriations committee

Several over-arching principles should guide public participation in the budget process. First, it is of fundamental importance that members of the public appropriate and use the opportunities for participation created by the new Act. This is particularly important when the origin, ownership and appropriateness of government economic policy is contested. It will require work to ensure that members of the public are aware of opportunities for participation, committee programming, and how best to develop and present a submission.

Secondly, meaningful public participation in budgeting will require input from wide-ranging and diverse sources. As shown by the case study above, this has not always been achieved.

Thirdly, there should be broad participation during each phase of the budget process in Parliament, and in the work of the appropriations and finance committees.

However, effective practice is as important as principle, and in this regard there is much work to be done by Parliament, civil society and members of the public. Seedat (2007b) suggests a number of practical ways in which Parliament could broaden public awareness, and solicit greater input, noting that when "Parliament goes about fulfilling its obligation to ensure public participation, it must ensure participation for all citizens: whether organised or unorganised, strong or lacking in influence". She suggests that barriers to participation, including language differences, geographical location and resources, should be addressed, and that draft legislation and other issues for debate in Parliament should be advertised more widely to the public. She also proposes that hearings should increasingly be held "outside of parliament precincts and especially in rural and marginalised areas" (Seedat, 2007b: 13).

Our case study also suggests that committees – including the new finance and appropriations committees – could take a more active role in soliciting and pursuing input from a wider spectrum of organisations that are under-represented in current debates, including academic institutions, labour unions and civil society organisations.

Fourthly, meaningful public participation in budgeting processes will undoubtedly require capacity development and support. For many, participating in the different phases of the budget process will be prohibitively time-consuming and costly. Members of the public and civil society organisations may require additional support in making submissions, as research points to relatively low levels of economic literacy and financial education in South Africa (Mbabane, 2004).

Such support should come partly from Parliament, but Seedat also suggests that civil society organisations and non-governmental organisations could "involve smaller and less well-resourced groups" in making submissions, "organising more joint research projects and the sharing of research facilities". She also points out that in the past, there has been proposals of "a room ... designated in Parliament itself for the express use of NGOs and other civil society organisations", although this has never been taken up. (Seedat, 2007b: 13-14).

Fifthly, there is room for substantial improvement in the way public input is captured and recorded. This is not a new concern, but it remains an administrative challenge for Parliament. As discussed above, committee reports on the sources and content of submissions appear inconsistent. Reports on submissions should be a standard, consistent output of public participation processes and should be widely available. The Report of the Independent Panel Assessment of Parliament also suggests that reports on public participation processes should be "debated within relevant committees and the plenary, leading ultimately to the adoption of resolutions", and recommends that "Parliament provides feedback to participating members of the public" (Independent Panel Assessment of Parliament, 2009: 54). Seedat also suggests that submission documents should be "filed, maintained and accessible", and that Parliament should "improve its record-keeping with regard to submissions, and statistical data on the number of bills and public hearings held annually" (Seedat, 2007b: 14).

Finally, and of crucial importance, meaningful participation will depend on Parliament's ability to receive, process and integrate public inputs into the budgeting process. Kass (2000) suggests that the perceived legitimacy of public participation processes will ultimately depend on the extent to which public input influences decision-making.

This will be a new challenge. Public inputs may be considered at present, but the Act is likely to mean that Parliament receives many more recommendations on budgetary allocations, and that more will be expected of their impact. The finance and appropriations committees will have to draw on the support and expertise of the proposed budget office in analysing and interpreting these submissions and making appropriate amendments.

6. POSSIBLE RISKS AND CHALLENGES OF PUBLIC PARTICIPATION

Parliament also faces risks associated with the new amendment powers and the broader mandate for participatory budgeting. It is possible that those with greater resources and an interest in shaping the budget will continue actively to exploit opportunities for public participation, drowning out other voices and generating a "consensus" which does not represent the interests of society at large. To some extent, this has already happened in the finance committee. Such interest groups could come from the private sector, but could also represent organised labour, civil society organisations and other social movements.

Critics have also warned that excessive public participation could delay budgetary decisions and jeopardise prudent fiscal policy. Heimans, for example, cautions that citizens and civil society organisations are often motivated by short-term interests without due regard for long-term budgetary consequences. He suggests that "participatory budgeting or public consultations simply result in 'shopping lists' of demands from communities that do not reflect the scarce resources available". He also argues that these processes could ultimately reduce "the quality of the decision outcome" (Heimans, in Moynihan, 2007: 82).

However, internationally there is little evidence linking the participation of citizens in budgetary processes and fiscal irresponsibility. In fact, budgets in which competing claims have been articulated and evaluated stand the best chance of being allocatively efficient and generating the highest social return. In addition, parliamentary oversight and amendment not only benefits from, but fundamentally requires, competing voices. As noted elsewhere in this book, the Act lays down a precise sequencing of amendments, which largely aims to ensure that proliferating amendments down the line do not jeopardise the sustainability of the budget in aggregate.

Arguably, Parliament's greatest challenge will be in ensuring the effective management of public participation in the context of new amendment powers. It will have to guard against the risk that expanded public participation will impose an "unreasonable" burden on committees in terms of cost, time and capacity. However, the Constitutional Court ruled in *Doctors for Life v Speaker of the National Assembly and Others* in 2006 that "reasonableness" requires that "appropriate account be paid to practicalities such as time and expense", but that the "saving of money and time in itself does not justify inadequate opportunities for public involvement".

7. CONCLUSION

The introduction of the Money Bills Amendment Procedure and Related Matters Act is an important development in meeting the requirements of the Constitution and bringing about a more participatory approach to budgeting in South Africa.

The inclusion of a number of dedicated opportunities for public participation will allow citizens to make an input into many different phases of the budget process in Parliament. And critically, the new amendment powers given to Parliament mean that public input could help shape the budget. However, the effectiveness of these opportunities for participation will ultimately depend on how well they are used.

The benefits of a more participatory budgeting approach include a deeper sense of public ownership of economic policy and greater confidence in the legitimacy and credibility of the state. But far more diverse and broad-based involvement will be required. Seedat suggests that participation should include all citizens "whether organised or unorganised, strong or lacking in influence" (Seedat, 2007b: 13).

To achieve broad and representative participation in budgeting, citizens will have to follow committee programmes and the work of Parliament; review budget proposals; make submissions; and hold MPs to account to ensure their inputs are considered.

However, active citizen participation in Parliament – and particularly in complex budgeting processes – will also require resources and support to improve the public's understanding of legislative processes, economic and policy literacy and capacity to make submissions. Parliament's newly adopted oversight model calls for the development of a public participation model, which should address the issue of support for citizens (Independent Panel Assessment of Parliament, 2009: 66). Seedat has suggested that there is also room for civil society organisations and academic institutions to work with "smaller and less well-resourced groups" (Seedat, 2007b: 13-14).

Without such support, there is a risk that the budgeting process will continue to be dominated by interest groups with significant resources and capacity, such as the private sector and industrial bodies and professional/sector associations. These organisations should not, of course, be excluded from participating. But it is important that their submissions are balanced by those of independent public interest organisations, and of individual citizens themselves.

REFERENCES

Bräutigam, D.A., "The People's Budget? Politics, Power, Popular Participation and Pro-Poor Economic Policy", revised draft paper prepared for the Expert Group Meeting on Participation of Civil Society in Fiscal Policy, Division for Public Administration and Development Management, Socio-Economic Governance and Management Branch, United Nations, New York, 16-17 March 2004. Available at: http://www2.ids.ac.uk/gdr/position%20papers/BrautigamParticBudgets.pdf

Bresser-Pereira, L.C., J. Maravall and A. Przeworski, *Economic Reform in New Democracies: A Social-Democratic Approach*, Cambridge, UK, Cambridge University Press, 1993.

Congress of South African Trade Unions (Cosatu), "COSATU demands proper consultation on budget", *COSATU Weekly*, 17 March 2006. Available at: http://www.cosatu.org.za/news/weekly/20060317.htm

De Lange, D., "Public pressure won't save Scorpions – ANC", *Pretoria News*, 31 July 2008, p 2. Available at: http://www.iol.co.za/index.php?set_id=1&click_id=13&art_id=vn20080731055734621C117245

De Villiers, S., "A Review of Public Participation in the Law and Policy-Making Process in South Africa", Parliamentary Support Programme, Parliament of South Africa, 2001. Available at: http://www.parliament.gov.za/live/content.php?Item_ID=285

Doctors for Life vs Speaker of the National Assembly and Others, 17 August 2006. Available at: www.constitutionalcourt.org.za.

February, J., "Drastic need for the public to have more say in the decisions of government", *Cape Times*, 10 August 2006. Available at: http://www.idasa.org

Friedman, S., "Participatory governance and citizen action in post-apartheid South Africa: Discussion Paper", International Institute of Labour Studies, 2006.

Hahndiek, P., Secretary of the Joint Budget Committee, Parliament of South Africa. Personal comment, December 2008.

Hickey, A. and A. van Zyl. "2002: South African Budget Guide and Dictionary" Idasa, 2002. Available at: http://www.idasa.org

Heimans, J., "Strengthening Participation in Public Expenditure Management: Policy Recommendations for Key Stakeholders", Paris, Organisation for Economic Co-operation and Development, 2002.

Independent Panel Assessment of Parliament, "Report of the Independent Panel Assessment of Parliament", Parliament of South Africa, 2009. Available at: http://www.parliament.gov.za.

Johnson, J.H. and S.S. Wasty, "Borrower Ownership of Adjustment Programs and the Political Economy of Reform," World Bank Discussion Paper No 199, Washington, DC: World Bank, 1993.

Kass, G., "Recent Developments in Public Participation in the United Kingdom", TA-Datenbank-Nachrichten, Nr. 3/9. Jahrgang - Oktober 2000, S. 20-28. Available at: http://www.itas.fzk.de/deu/tadn/tadn003/kass00a.htm

Krafchik, W., "The participation of civil society and legislatures in the formulation of the budget", in Houston, G. (ed.), *Public participation in democratic governance in South Africa*, Pretoria: Human Sciences Research Council, 2001.

Lefko-Everett, K., 2009. "Promoting citizen participation in the South African Public Service", *Journal of the Public Service Commission*, forthcoming.
– "Money Bill giving MPs a say in budget process also demands greater diligence", *Cape Times*, 6 November 2008, p 11.

Levin, R., 2004. "Building service effectiveness: Integrated governance and the developmental state," *Service Delivery Review* Vol 3 No 1, p 31. Available at: http://www.dpsa.gov.za/documents/service_delivery_review/Vol3ed1/SDR_Vol

Mbabane, L., "The end is far from nigh", *Mail & Guardian*, 26 January 2004.

Moynihan, D.P., "Citizen Participation in Budgeting: Prospects for Developing Countries," in Shah, A. (ed.), *Public Sector Governance and Accountability: Participatory Budgeting*, Washington, D.C., World Bank, 2007.

Murray, C. and L. Nijzink, "Building Representative Democracy – South Africa's Legislatures and the Constitution", Parliamentary Support Programme, Parliament of South Africa, 2002.

National Treasury, "Treasury Guidelines and 2008 Budget Process", 2007. Available at: http://www.treasury.gov.za.

Parliament of South Africa, Available at: www.parliament.gov.za.

Parliamentary Monitoring Group. Available at: www.pmg.org.za.

Parliamentary Monitoring Group. "Private Members' Legislative Proposals and Special Pensions: Standing Committee, Mrs C Kellerman's Petition, 9 November 2005." Available at: http://www.pmg.org.za/minutes/20051108-kellerman-petition

People's Budget Coalition. "Budgeting for surplus in the midst of poverty, inequality and unemployment: People's Budget Campaign Proposals 2009-2010", 2009. Available at: http://www.sangoco.org.za/images/stories/Pdf_Documents/PBC_2009_Proposals_FinalToPrint2008.pdf

Public Service Commission, State of the Public Service Report 2008, Pretoria: Public Service Commission. Available at: http://www.psc.gov.za/docs/reports/2008/SOPS%20Report.pdf.

Ramkumar, V., "Our Money, Our Responsibilty: A Citizens' Guide to Monitoring Government Expenditure", Washington, D.C., International Budget Project, 2008.

SABiNet, "Bill accedes to Kellerman parliamentary petition on pension rights", 24 October 2008. Available at: http://www.sabinet.co.za/sabinetlaw/news_par849.html

Seedat, S., "Separating people from decisions that affect them",Business Day, 13 September 2007a. Available at: Available at http://www.businessday.co.za/articles/opinion.aspx?ID=BD4A563289.

– "The Ethos of Law-Making: Participatory Democracy and Public Involvement in Law-Making: Lessons from the Constitutional Court of South Africa", Idasa, July 2007b.

UN Habitat online. Available at: http://ww2.unhabitat.org/cdrom/TRANSPARENCY/html/2d_7.html

Vavi, W., "Editorial", The Shopsteward, Vol 7 No 1, February 1998. Available at: http://www.cosatu.org.za/shop/shop0701.htm

Verwey, L. and K. Lefko-Everett, "MTBPS 2007", Idasa, 2007. Available at: http://www.idasa.org

APPENDIX 1:
CONSTITUTIONAL PROVISIONS
ON MONEY BILLS

77. MONEY BILLS [ORIGINAL VERSION]

(1)   A Bill that appropriates money or imposes taxes, levies or duties is a money Bill. A money Bill may not deal with any other matter except a subordinate matter incidental to the appropriation of money or the imposition of taxes, levies or duties.

(2)   All money Bills must be considered in accordance with the procedure established by section 75. An Act of Parliament must provide for a procedure to amend money Bills before Parliament.

Source: Constitution of the Republic of South Africa, Act No. 108 of 1996.

77. MONEY BILLS [AS AMENDED]

(1)   A Bill is a money Bill if it—
  (a)   appropriates money;
  (b)   imposes national taxes, levies, duties or surcharges;
  (c)   abolishes or reduces, or grants exemptions from, any national taxes, levies, duties or surcharges; or
  (d)   authorises direct charges against the National Revenue Fund, except a Bill envisaged in section 214 authorising direct charges.

(2)   A money Bill may not deal with any other matter except—
  (a)   a subordinate matter incidental to the appropriation of money;
  (b)   the imposition, abolition or reduction of national taxes, levies, duties or surcharges;
  (c)   the granting of exemption from national taxes, levies, duties or surcharges; or
  (d)   the authorisation of direct charges against the National Revenue Fund.

(3)   All money Bills must be considered in accordance with the procedure established by section 75. An Act of Parliament must provide for a procedure to amend money Bills before Parliament.

Source: Constitution of the Republic of South Africa, Act No. 108 of 1996, as amended by the Constitution of the Republic of South Africa Second Amendment Act, Act No. 61 of 2001.

Appendix 2:
Principles for amending the fiscal framework and money bills in South Africa's new legislation

When amending the fiscal framework, a money Bill or taking any decision in terms of this Act, Parliament and its committees must —

(a)   ensure that there is an appropriate balance between revenue, expenditure and borrowing;

(b)   ensure that debt levels and debt interest cost are reasonable;

(c)   ensure that the cost of recurrent spending is not deferred to future generations;

(d)   ensure that there is adequate provision for spending on infrastructure development, overall capital spending and maintenance;

(e)   consider the short, medium and long-term implications of the fiscal framework, division of revenue and national budget on the long-term growth potential of the economy and the development of the country;

(f)   take into account cyclical factors that may impact on the prevailing fiscal position; and

(g)   take into account all public revenue and expenditure, including extra-budgetary funds, and contingent liabilities.

Source: Money Bills Amendment Procedure and Related Matters Act [NO 9, 2009].

ENDNOTES

1 The following organisations made submissions at the hearings: the Business Parliamentary Office, the People's Budget Campaign, Idasa, AFReC, the National Treasury, Black Sash, Ernst & Young, the South African Institute of Chartered Accountants, the Financial and Fiscal Commission and the Federation of Unions of South Africa.

Chapter One

2 Delgerjargal Uvsh and Brian Weeks provided valuable research assistance for Chapter 1 during their time as interns at Idasa.

3 Allocative efficiency refers to the extent to which allocations match the preferences of households; operational efficiency refers to the extent to which allocations are spent with a minimum of waste. Both efficiency criteria need to be met for the budget to have maximum impact. In this chapter it is assumed that poorer households receive a higher weighting in calculating the budget's utility-enhancement. That is, it is assumed that allocative efficiency requires some degree of redistributive incidence in allocations.

4 cf. "Expanding the Social Security Net in South Africa: Opportunities, Challenges and Constraints", Pauw, K. and Mncube, L., *International Poverty Centre Country Study*, Number 8, July 2007.

5 cf. *Development as Freedom*, Amartya Sen, Oxford University Press, especially chapter 4.

6 That is, freedom understood not only as freedom from oppression, deprivation and the like, but to pursue aspirations.

7 The United Nations' Human Development Index is probably the best-known attempt to conceive and measure development in a broader sense than mere income adequacy. The index consists of per capita income, life expectancy and educational attainment.

8 A recent report by the South African presidency defines poverty in a way that brings together some of the relevant issues: "Poverty is understood as deficiency in an individual's socio-economic capabilities. Its manifestations include factors such as income, access to basic services, access to assets, information, social networks or social capital. This broad approach to poverty allows for engagement with the reality of poverty and the combination of things that should be done to deal with it." (South African Government, 2008: 4).

9 cf. especially chapter 5 on public participation in budgeting.

10 In Africa and Latin America especially, many such reforms are associated with highly divisive structural adjustment programmes as conditions for receiving IMF and World Bank loans. The issue of "ownership" of the budget is, therefore, significant. Though South Africa has been largely insulated from direct pressure from these multilateral institutions, some commentators would argue that more subtle pressures resulted in a self-imposed structural adjustment programme from 1996 to 2001. This may have had similar adverse consequences, including implications for the degree of "ownership" of the fiscal policy stance.

11 "Budget system" refers to the totality of players and processes in budgeting, and is distinguished from budget policy, which refers more narrowly to the indication of intended spending and revenue for a given period.

12 For case-studies on aspects of the budget system in selected African countries cf. Idasa 2005 *Budget Transparency and Participation 2: Nine African Case Studies*. The Open Budget Index of the Centre for

Budget and Policy Priorities is a very useful and rigorously conceived evaluation of budget "openness" in more than 100 countries.

13 For useful reviews of the budgeting challenges facing many developing countries, as well as some developed countries, cf. *Spend and Deliver: The Medium-Term Expenditure Framework*, Walker, L. and Mengistu B. The authors also provide a useful discussion of budgeting approaches and their respective challenges.

14 A good budget well implemented is of course the ideal: a bad budget badly implemented may in some contexts have less of a negative impact than a bad budget that is implemented well!

15 Since preferences vary between voters, this requirement is sometimes rephrased in terms of the preferences of the median voter. The challenges associated with aligning preferences and public spending and taxation have been thoroughly explored in the literature on public choice, following seminal contributions such as those of Buchanan, J. and Tullock, G., in *The Calculus of Consent*.

16 It is an interesting question whether a "good" budget from a democratic perspective is often a "bad" budget from a macro-economic perspective. The literature on the risks of macro-economic populism in many ways stems from a fear of excessive participation, particularly in societies marked by social tension and inequality. Chapter 5 on public participation further touches on this question. Rodrik (1997), in "Democracy and Economic Performance", provides an empirical refutation of the association between democratic participation and poor economic performance.

17 Trust and networks of association are assets that are built up over time and can also be eroded. Higher levels of social capital benefit people who can access them in a range of ways.

18 This echoes the "consensual" approach associated with the corporatist model of policy-making, which in South Africa has found limited expression in Nedlac. It is worth noting that countries who have successfully used such a model are in most, if not all, cases characterised by comparatively high levels of social capital.

19 cf. *MTBPS 2006: Parliament. ASGISA and Infrastructure*, Idasa, pp. 3-6

20 cf. Faulkner, D. and Loeweld, C., "Policy Change and Economic Growth: A Case Study of South Africa" and Ajam, T. and Aron, J., "Fiscal Renaissance in a Democratic South Africa".

21 cf. Van der Berg, S., "Fiscal Expenditure Incidence in South Africa: A Report for the National Treasury", 2005.

22 The availability of data and the uncertain and still evolving impact of the global contraction made it advisable to evaluate trends up to, but not beyond, mid-2008 at the time of writing.

23 Further results of these studies are not summarised here, but can be found in the papers themselves, including breakdowns by province and factors such as race. This chapter also cannot do justice to some of the current debates and controversies on poverty measurement and the comparability of various data sets in South Africa. cf. Bhorat, H. and Kanbur, R. (2006), and Stats SA (2000).

24 A third possible reason, namely significant increases in eligible beneficiaries as a result of increases in poverty, is unlikely to have played a large role. Adjustment of eligibility criteria here refers mainly to increasing the eligibility age for the child support grant (now 14) and smaller adjustments to the old age grant. Further upward adjustments have been proposed. Until recently, there has been little adjustment of the income dimension of the means test, even for inflation, with the result that, in real terms, the means criteria became more stringent between 2001 and 2008. Not adjusting the means test for inflation has presumably been a way of keeping grant spending in check. Interestingly, this suggests that the authorities significantly underestimated poverty in South Africa when the initial grant parameters were set and beneficiary estimates and financing requirements were determined.

25 cf. Pauw, K. and Mncube, L., 2007, *Expanding the Social Security Net in South Africa: Opportunities, Challenges and Constraints*.

26 This study is useful because the approach uses survey methods to generate a list of essentials and then determines poverty with reference to them by looking at the percentage of households that lack goods and services that are considered essential across a wide range of income groups.

27 cf. *The Open Budget Index*, 2009, where South Africa scored second highest out of more than a 100 developed and developing countries.

28 The extent to which advocacy by interest groups has influenced budgets through formal participatory channels is, however, more difficult to determine. In the absence, until recently, of formal budget amendment power, it was always possible to argue that such participation largely had the function of legitimising foregone conclusions. Issues of public participation are discussed in detail in chapter five.

29 cf. *Parliament, ASGISA and Infrastructure*, Idasa, 2006

30 It is doubtful, however, that changes to the priorities represented by budget allocations are best pursued through advocacy in February, when the budget is tabled. Parliament and civil society would be far better served by taking a truly medium-term approach to budgeting. This would mean advocating now, on the strength of sound research, for changes in so-called "outer year" budgets. This point is emphasised again in the conclusion of this chapter.

31 cf. for example *Framework for Managing Programme Performance Information*, National Treasury,

32 Not all private care is clinically superior or more attentive to patients' need to have their dignity respected. The fact that such strong perceptions persist, however, is something of an indictment of public health in South Africa and a basic challenge for health departments and practitioners, overseen by legislatures.

33 There is an additional reason for using financial information at this stage. Though National Treasury recently released the framework for managing programme performance information, the legal status of this document is unclear.

34 cf. Idasa "Budget 2009: Still Getting the Balance Right?" as well as Idasa, "Trends in 2006/2007 Departmental Expenditure: Submission to the Joint Budget Committee".

Chapter Two

35 Section 120 applied similar provisions to the nine provinces. Here, one striking exception was the review of the appropriation bill by the Mpumalanga legislature in 1997, the first year in which the newly created provinces were responsible for developing their own budgets. The legislature's finance committee discovered that the provincial budget as tabled by the executive was unbalanced. It embarked on an unprecedented reprioritisation exercise and identified spending cuts. At one stage, the member of the executive council (MEC) for finance and his officials walked out of the legislature in protest against a R59-million cut in his departmental budget, only to be forced to return and apologise. The process resulted in the first and only occasion on which a provincial legislature introduced a new appropriation bill (Newham 1997).

36 The 1999 Public Finance Management Act regulates the timing of budgets (section 27), expenditure before the annual budget is passed (section 29), and virement within votes (section 43).

37 The Department of Finance tabled the Treasury Control Bill in 1998. The finance committee formed a sub-committee to rewrite the bill, which met numerous times over several months, including during two parliamentary recesses, and produced 22 consecutive amendment-capturing drafts. Those

involved joked about renaming the bill the "Woods-Momoniat Memorial Bill" (Feinstein 2007: 71), to honour the two principal individuals who guided the process, an MP and a Treasury official respectively. In the end, they settled for a more prosaic title.

38 The committee's schedule of sessions on the 2003 budget started with a "training" session run by the National Treasury on how to interpret the estimates of national expenditure.

39 The political committee is charged with providing strategic direction to the party in Parliament and liaising with the ANC's National Working Committee.

40 Section 10(5)(a) of the version of the bill tabled by the finance committee had stipulated that "no more than 10 percent of the funds appropriated for a main division within a vote, excluding projected personnel costs, may be appropriated conditionally".

Chapter Three

41 This cabinet sub-committee, chaired by the minister of finance, provides ongoing political guidance at various key points in the budget cycle.

42 For instance, in *Government of the Republic of South Africa and Others v Grootboom and Others* 2000, the court ordered government to set aside a "reasonable proportion" of its housing budget for short-term relief.

43 This forms one of the constitutional bases for the Public Finance Management Act of 1999.

44 Allocative efficiency pertains to the ability of the budget system to distribute scarce public resources in terms of government priorities. In this context, it ensures that, through effective prioritisation, a given quantum of public funds results in the greatest social welfare.

45 Director-Generals are political appointees. Once a DG has told a minister to put in writing a directive with financial implications, he or she might as well start applying for a new job.

46 The Budget Council is an example of this, before it was formalised in legislation.

47 *Minister of Health and Others v Treatment Action Campaign and Others* 2002 (10) BCLR) 1033 (CC).

Chapter Four

48 For example, the fiscal framework needs to be passed or amended before the division of revenue is considered, which in turn needs to be passed or amended to remain consistent with this adopted framework.

49 cf. Verwey (2008)

Chapter Five

50 Formerly the Joint Budget Committee.

51 The authors acknowledge the possibility of some error, including the possible omission of some records or reports, or notes from specific meetings. The analysis included submissions, as well as expert opinions, often solicited in response to the budget. Presentations by departments and legal opinions sought in reference to specific legislation were excluded.

52 This category largely comprised umbrella bodies representing professional or sector interests, including such bodies as the Actuarial Society of South Africa, the Association of Chartered Certified Accountants and the Banking Association of South Africa.

www.ingramcontent.com/pod-product-compliance
Lightning Source LLC
Chambersburg PA
CBHW080000280326
41935CB00013B/1705